The Prime Minister
— and —
His Mistress

Sir Oliver Popplewell

Copyright © 2014 Sir Oliver Popplewell.

Photograph acknowledgments to Pitt Rivers

All rights reserved. No part of this book may be reproduced, stored, or transmitted by any means—whether auditory, graphic, mechanical, or electronic—without written permission of both publisher and author, except in the case of brief excerpts used in critical articles and reviews. Unauthorized reproduction of any part of this work is illegal and is punishable by law.

ISBN: 978-1-4834-1431-7 (sc)
ISBN: 978-1-4834-1429-4 (hc)
ISBN: 978-1-4834-1430-0 (e)

Library of Congress Control Number: 2014912298

Because of the dynamic nature of the Internet, any web addresses or links contained in this book may have changed since publication and may no longer be valid. The views expressed in this work are solely those of the author and do not necessarily reflect the views of the publisher, and the publisher hereby disclaims any responsibility for them.

Any people depicted in stock imagery provided by Thinkstock are models, and such images are being used for illustrative purposes only.
Certain stock imagery © Thinkstock.

Lulu Publishing Services rev. date: 7/17/2014

For Liz

CONTENTS

1. The Background 1
2. The Prime Minister 7
3. Venetia 37
4. Montagu 49
5. The Nature of the Relationship 77
6. Venetia's Subsequent Behaviour 93
7. The Language and Volume of the Correspondence 99
8. Confidential Information and Advice 107
9. The Conspiracy of Silence 121
10. Opportunities 129
11. The Verdict 135

Asquith Venetia & Violet

CHAPTER 1

The Background

Perhaps in this day and age, a sixty-year-old married man writing love letters to a twenty-year-old girl is not in itself very remarkable. But the author of the letters, Herbert Henry Asquith, had been prime minister of Britain since April 1908. He had been married twice. In 1877, at the age of twenty-four, he first married Helen Melland, and they had five children. She died of typhoid fever in the summer of 1891. Before that, he had been writing love letters to Margot Tennant, whom he married on 10 May 1894. His daughter Violet by his first marriage, later Violet Bonham Carter, was a contemporary of Venetia Stanley, the youngest daughter of Lord Sheffield. Venetia was the recipient of Asquith's letters. The letters started before the First World War, which began in 1914, but gathered pace during the war until they ceased in 1915. Although he was in charge of a government, which in peacetime had been beset with political problems and was now involved in a global war, Asquith had no difficulty in devoting his attentions to Venetia. This, then, was background to their affair.

Like all governments, the Liberal administration, who had defeated the Conservatives in 1906, and of which Asquith was a leading member, had constant political problems, the most pressing of which, before the outbreak of war, was the question of Ulster. This was a century-old dispute between the Protestant province of Ulster and the Catholic provinces in Ireland, which sought independence from British rule. Ulster had dominated the political landscape ever since the Liberals had sought to introduce home rule bills in 1886, 1893, and 1912. However, the solution to the problem was postponed by the outbreak of the war in August 1914, which raised different but no less intractable difficulties. The major question now was how to overcome the deadlock on the Western Front in France, where the rival armies faced each other from entrenched positions.

When the war started, people confidently expected that it would be over by Christmas, but far from there being a speedy resolution of the fighting in France, by Christmas 1914 there was a stalemate on the Western Front. Plans were therefore prepared to break the deadlock by opening up the Dardanelles, the waterway to Constantinople, capital of Turkey, now Germany's ally, in the belief that it would help the Russians, knock Turkey out of the war, and provide a threat to Germany in the Balkans. The dispute between the "Westerners" who favoured fighting in France and the "Easterners" who preferred war in the Balkans and the Dardanelles lasted until 1915.

The attack on the Dardanelles started with a naval bombardment in December 1914. By March 1915, the naval approach to the Dardanelles had failed. The decision was taken to replace the naval strategy by landing troops at Gallipoli. This also failed.

Elsewhere the war was going badly. In February 1915, the Germans had started a U-boat campaign. In the East, the Russians were on the retreat, having suffered heavy casualties in battles with the Germans. On the Western Front, there was continued stalemate and also an ever-increasing number of casualties without material gain.

None of these wartime setbacks, most of which involved life-and-death decisions, had been allowed to interfere with Asquith's penchant for writing a flood of passionate letters to Venetia. In the period between August 1914 and May 1915, he wrote her some 350 letters. Although his letters have survived, only a few of hers to him have been found. On one occasion, he wrote four letters to her in one day. Some seem to have been written during cabinet meetings, a practice that had started before the outbreak of the war. Some were written while Asquith was at the House of Commons, during debates. After the war started, some letters were also written during War Council meetings. The correspondence between Asquith and Venetia, which starting in 1912 had effectively become daily, ceased in May 1915, when Venetia announced her engagement to Edwin Montagu, Asquith's former private secretary. On 26 July 1915, Edwin and Venetia were married.

The war in France started with a German invasion of Northern France and Belgium. From 14 August until 25 August 1914, British and French troops were engaged in a series of battles with the Germans, who had advanced to the Belgian frontier and into northern Flanders. The first encounter between British and German troops occurred on 22 August, at Soignies, when the British Expeditionary Force (BEF) was moving toward Charleroi in order to join up with the French Fifth Army. The BEF then took up position on the Mons Canal. The Battle of Mons started on 23 August, when the German First Army under General von Kluck attacked the BEF.

However, the French Fifth Army, which had been routed by the Germans at Sambre on 22 August and was meant to be guarding the British right flank, now withdrew. As a result, there was a long retreat by the BEF to the River Marne on 24 August. On the same day, Field Marshal Sir John French, the commander-in-chief of the BEF, had sent Field Marshal Lord Kitchener, the Secretary of State for War, a telegram marked "secret". In it he set out details of the retreat and the precise lines of defence that the BEF and the Fifth French Army were about to take up. Kitchener passed on the telegram to Asquith who, on the same day, enclosed it in a letter that he was writing to Venetia. He added, "I wish we had something like a code that we could use by the telegraph. This morning, for instance, I longed to let you know, before anyone else, what had happened and was happening". Asquith seems to have had no qualms about passing on secret information to Venetia during the war and asking for her advice.

The retreat culminated in the battle of Le Cateau on 26 August. The French lost a third of a million men, and British casualties were also high. On 28 August, Maurice Bonham Carter wrote from France to Violet, whom he subsequently married, "Our troops have no doubt lost heavily as they had to retire in the face of very heavy artillery fire and I fear some of our guns have been lost. Do not mention this. I expect that by this time that we must have had about 10,000 casualties."[1]

It was, as the *Sunday Times* reported on 30 August, nothing less than a disaster for the BEF. The newspaper's headline read "Broken British Regiments Battling against Odds." The article was written by Arthur Moore, who, with Henry Hamilton Fyfe of the *Daily Mail*, had managed to visit the troops at Amiens and found out the full extent of the defeat. The main article read, "Our losses are very great. I have seen the broken bits of many regiments … there is no failure of discipline, no panic, no throwing up the sponge … the men are battered with marching … to sum up, the first great German effort has succeeded. We have to face the fact that the BEF, which bore the great weight of the blow, has suffered terrible losses and requires immediate and immense reinforcement."[2]

The British and the French were divided on tactics. Venetia soon learned of the strained relations between [Sir John] French and General Joffre, the commander-in-chief of the French Army. In his letter of 31 August, Asquith wrote, "We had bad news this morning from [Sir John] French. Joffre was in favour of a further retirement of the French Armies, and wished French to remain practically where he was. French took umbrage at this, and proposes, himself, to retire behind the Seine, basing himself on La Rochelle. We all think this is quite wrong (all this *most secret*)."

The state of the war in France while he was writing this letter was described by the military correspondent of the *Times* who reported:

> "The situation is not brilliant but it is not bad. The Anglo-French Armies are lucky to be quit of their difficulties without a very serious reverse, without their front being broken and without great loss of efficiency and prestige.

---

[1] Violet Bonham Carter, *Champion Redoubtable*, ed. Mark Pottle (London: Weidenfeld & Nicholson, 1998), 7.

[2] Arthur Moore, "Broken British Regiments Battling against Odds", *Sunday Times*, 30 August, 1914.

> Recrimination concerning past faults is as useless as it is unnecessary. The main thing for the Allies now to do, as President Poincare rightly says, is to endure and fight.... The enemy has marched far and fast ... it will take us a good three years to create the military instrument, which we require, to bring the Germans to book; if this long war involves us in unparalleled suffering and expense, we must remember that we deliberately chose the path we have pursued."[3]

Despite the horrendous effects of the war, at midnight on 30 December 30 1914, Asquith was able to write, "This year has been, in the fullest sense, what the Ancients used to call 'annus mirabilis' – to you and me – it has been a succession of marvellous experiences." Given his background, how did it come about that Asquith, now Prime Minister, should entrust Venetia with so many secrets and rely on her advice about important political matters?

---

3   *Times*, 4 September, 1914, 6.

CHAPTER TWO

The Prime Minister

Asquith was born in September 1852, on the same day the great Duke of Wellington died. The widespread grief which engulfed the country did not affect the birth of Asquith at Croft House, Morley, in the West Riding of Yorkshire. Croft House was a substantial six-bedroom stone house, with a coach house, various cottages and barns, and a magnificent view over the dales towards Leeds.

Queen Victoria was less than halfway through her reign. Petrol engines were unknown. Steam engines were in their infancy. Steamships were still something of a rarity. The Battle of Waterloo was still in the memory of a large proportion of the adult population. Electricity scarcely existed. By April 1915, when Asquith's relationship with Venetia came to an end, the world into which he was born had changed out of all recognition. France was now an ally. Half the globe was coloured pink to denote the British possessions all over the world. The industrial revolution, which was the hallmark of the latter part of the nineteenth century, had transformed a predominantly agricultural Europe into a manufacturing conglomerate, capable of producing not merely the necessities of life, but an exciting and innovative range of inventions, which were to transform the lives of many.

Asquith started life with no particular patronage on which to rely. His successes were almost entirely self-achieved. Certainly, no one could have achieved what Asquith did without a certain amount of luck. But it was in recognising and seizing the chances before him that for Asquith made the difference between success and failure. Asquith's father worked in the woollen trade in Morley, in the West Riding of Yorkshire. He died at the age of 35 of some intestinal problem while playing cricket. Asquith had an older brother, William, who, because of an injury to his spine while playing games at school, never grew much beyond five foot and spent the rest of his life after Oxford as a schoolmaster at Clifton College.

Asquith also had three sisters, two of whom died young. He and his brother had been taught by their mother until the death of their father, after which the family were supported by their uncle, William Willans. The family moved to Huddersfield, where Willans ran a wool stapling business. There, Asquith and his brother went to school. Two years later, when Willans died, the family moved again, this time to St Leonards in Sussex, where they went to live with another uncle, John Willans, who took charge of their education. Both brothers went to the City of London School, where Asquith became head of the school and won one of only two classical open scholarships to Balliol College, Oxford. Balliol, then as now, had a formidable reputation for classical scholarship. It was a remarkable achievement for a boy from a minor school to have succeeded in competition with other boys from more distinguished public schools. He went up to Oxford in October 1870, at the same time as the new master, the famous Benjamin Jowett.

At Oxford, Asquith had a distinguished academic career. He got a first in Moderations (informally called Mods) in 1872, and was runner-up in the Hertford Scholarship. He was twice runner-up for the Ireland Prize ("for the promotion of classical learning and taste"), and on the second occasion, in 1874, he was awarded a special consolation prize because of the narrowness of his defeat. He subsequently obtained a first in Literae Humaniores (Greats), and shared the Craven Scholarship. In his last term, as a Liberal,[4] he became president of the Union, having previously been treasurer. He was elected a fellow of his college. It was by most standards a remarkable achievement, though Roy Jenkins (a

---

4 The Liberals and the Conservatives were effectively the only political parties at this time.

distinguished politician and author) observed "that his successes were striking without being sensational and ... were achieved on the basis of a moderate and controlled amount of work."[5]

After coming down from Oxford and before taking up his fellowship, he became tutor to the son of the Earl of Portsmouth. Thereafter, and for the next year, he remained at Balliol. He continued to keep his fellowship for another five years, but in 1875 decided to become a lawyer in London. Many years later, his attachment to Oxford was exemplified by his decision upon being ennobled in 1925 to take the title of Earl of Oxford and Asquith. This did not prevent the alumni of Oxford in the same year, owing to some petty jealousy or spite, from defeating his candidature for the chancellorship of the university. In the same way, many years later, the university declined to award an honorary degree to Margaret Thatcher because of its dislike of her educational policies.

In order to practise at the bar, Asquith had to join an inn and to eat dinners. There are four Inns of Court: Inner Temple, Middle Temple, Lincoln's Inn, and Gray's Inn. Historically, they were like colleges, and every prospective barrister had to join one. Eating dinners required the barrister to attend the inn over a period of time to introduce him to life at the bar. Asquith joined Lincoln's Inn, and in October 1875 became a pupil of Charles Bowen at Brick Court. A pupil, as the word indicates, is attached to a barrister and learns his skills from his master. A good pupil-master will be of immense value to a pupil because some of the skills of a good master will inevitably pass down to the pupil. So it was with Asquith and Bowen. Barristers are self-employed and are grouped in chambers together but are independent. Pupillage usually lasts for twelve months, at the end of which the pupil may be lucky enough to become a tenant (a permanent member of chambers). Somewhat unusually, Asquith became a pupil before he was called to the bar, which was in June 1876. In those less regimented days, it was possible to become a pupil without filling in endless forms or having interminable interviews. It was a matter of patronage. Chambers were very small,

---

5   Roy Jenkins, *Asquith* (London: Collins, 1964), 23.

often consisting of no more than half a dozen tenants and perhaps a single pupil. Modern chambers with up to seventy or eighty tenants were unknown, but the difficulties facing a young barrister then, in getting started, remain the same today.

Asquith was able to obtain pupillage because Bowen, who had been Dr Arnold's prize pupil at Rugby, had himself also been a scholar at Balliol, a fellow while still an undergraduate, and president of the Union. Bowen was a highly distinguished advocate. He, too, had had a meteoric career, though not perhaps as a jury advocate. There is an apocryphal story that once when he prosecuted a man found on the roof of a building with a burglar's tool kit, he said to the jury in an ironical tone, "If you consider, gentlemen, that the accused was on the roof of the house for the purpose of enjoying the midnight breezes, and by pure accident, happened to have about him the necessary tools of the housebreaker with no dishonest intention of employing them, you will, of course, acquit him." The irony was lost on the jury who proceeded to find the accused not guilty.[6]

At the time of Asquith's pupillage, Bowen was aged 41. He had just finished appearing as counsel in the celebrated Tichborne case. Roger Tichborne was the son of a famous Catholic family who was brought up in Paris. After leaving Stonyhurst and entering the army, he went to South America in 1853. In 1854 he boarded the *Bella* to sail from New York to Brazil. The *Bella* vanished and its longboat was found adrift. Tichborne was presumed dead in 1855. In 1862 his father died. His mother refused to believe in her son's death and caused enquiries to be made about him abroad. As a result, she was told that a man answering to Tichborne's description was living in Wagga Wagga, New South Wales, and working as a butcher. In fact, he was Arthur Orton, a butcher from Wapping who spoke no French and bore little physical resemblance to Tichborne. However, supplied with money by Tichborne's distraught mother, Orton came to Europe, visited her in Paris, and persuaded her that he was the missing heir to the estates. Others came forward to support Orton's claim.

---

6   Douglas Woodruff, *The Tichborne Claimant* (London: Hollis and Carter, 1957), 170.

The Prime Minister and His Mistress

The case involved two lengthy trials, the first of which was a civil trial. It started in 1871 and lasted some 102 days. It was concerned with establishing whether Orton was the rightful heir to the Tichborne estate. He was discredited in the witness box by Sir John Coleridge, QC, who was leading Bowen, among others, for the Tichborne family. The claimant had difficulty in giving an account of life at Stonyhurst school where Tichborne had been educated. Although Orton claimed that he could make out Greek letters and read Latin, he did not know whether Caesar had written in prose or verse or whether he was a Latin or Greek writer. He rather thought he was Greek. He was handed a copy of Virgil but did not know who he was, whether it was prose or poetry, or whether it was in Latin or Greek. He believed that he had read Euclid. He was then asked:

Q: "Did you ever hear of the Asses' bridge?

A: I do not recollect.

Q: Did you ever try to cross the Asses' bridge?

A: I do not know. Probably I did.

Q: Did anybody try to help you over the Asses' bridge?

A: I have no recollection of it.

Q: You do not know what it is?

A: I have no recollection.

Q: Do you know whereabouts it is … how far from Stonyhurst?

A: I can put up with all your insulting.

Q: Do you know it under its Latin title? Perhaps that would bring it home to you: *pons assinorum*?

A: I have no recollection.

Q: You cannot recollect anybody doing his very best to help you over that structure?

A: I should advise you to joke a little less over this."[7]

The only surprise about the case is that it took so long before the jury announced that they did not require to hear any further evidence. The claimant elected not to proceed further. This brought the civil action to a close. In 1873, Orton was prosecuted for perjury in a second trial. This lasted 180 days. He was convicted and sentenced to fourteen years penal servitude.

Bowen was at that time *Treasury Devil*. This is a position held by a junior counsel, usually for no more than five years. There are two categories of barristers: junior counsel and Queen's Counsel. The word "junior" does not refer to age, merely that the person so described is not a Queen's Counsel. The position of Treasury Devil is a prestigious Government appointment. It involves advising and representing the Crown in its major civil litigation. At the end of his appointment as the Treasury Devil, it is customary for the holder of the office to be promoted to the High Court Bench without becoming a QC. In addition to his work on behalf of the Crown, the Treasury Devil was in those days allowed to have a private practice. At the young age of 44, Bowen went to the High Court Bench. He was a *puisne* judge for only three years, sat in the Court of Appeal for eleven years, and ended his judicial career as a Law Lord in the House of Lords.

It is a great advantage to a pupil (then as now) to be taken on at the end of his or her pupillage as a tenant in the same chambers. The

---

7   Viscount Maugham, *The Tichborne Case* (London: Hodder and Stoughton, 1936), 222–223, 226.

pupil's familiarity with the work there, his previous introduction to chambers' solicitors, and the prospect of work flowing down from other members of chambers gives an ex-pupil some advantage in starting his own practice.

This was not to be Asquith's path. The reasons for his not obtaining tenancy at the end of his pupillage are not known. Asquith's memoirs are strangely silent on the matter, although it is suggested that Bowen already had an understudy.[8] Asquith then moved for a short while to 1 Hare Court. Why he went there in the first place, and why he left soon after joining is also not known. But he did, and he went to 6 Fig Tree Court. He was joined there by two of Bowen's other former pupils, Henry Cunynghame and Mark Napier, who had been at Wellington College together.

Unsurprisingly, three recently called barristers, without any connections and without more senior members to help, could command little work. Thus, Asquith suffered the familiar fate of countless members of the bar, both before and after his time, of simply sitting around doing nothing, while waiting for that elusive brief. It is difficult to conceive of a more dispiriting way of life for any young man, and more so for someone with Asquith's distinguished academic background. He did this for some six years, supported financially to a limited extent by his Balliol fellowship. As other penniless barristers have done, he also taught, lectured, marked exam papers, and wrote articles for the *Economist* and for the *Spectator*. He needed the money, because in August 1887 he married Helen Melland.

They had four sons: Raymond, born in 1878; Herbert (Bec), born in 1881; Arthur (Oc), born in 1883; and Cryil (Cys), born in 1890. They also had one daughter, Violet (later, Lady Violet Bonham Carter), born in 1887. It was her friendship with Venetia which was the catalyst for Asquith's own relationship with Venetia.

Asquith's description of his marriage to Helen is rather movingly contained in a long letter he wrote to Mrs (later Lady) Horner on 11 September 1892, the first anniversary of his wife's death.

---

8   Spender & Asquith, *Life of Henry Herbert Asquith* (London: Hutchinson & Co., !932), i. 40.

"She had one of those personalities which it is almost impossible to depict. The strong colours of the palette seem to be too heavy and garish; it is difficult to paint a picture in the soft grey tints which would best suit her, and yet she was not neutral or negative. Her mind was clear and strong, but it was not cut in facets and did not flash lights, and no one would call her clever or "intellectual." What gave her, her rare quality was her character, which everyone who knew her intimately (Haldane for instance) agrees, was the most selfless and unworldly that they have ever encountered. She was warm, impulsive, naturally quick tempered, and generous almost to a fault. She cared little for society, shrank from every kind of publicity and self advertisement, hardly knew what ambition meant.... She was the gentlest and best of companions, a restricting rather than a stimulating influence, and knowing myself as I do, I have often wondered that we walked so evenly together."[9]

The picture which he there portrays of his first wife is that she was something of a mouse who did not share Asquith's enjoyment of a wide social life. Their son Cyril described her. "She was completely unworldly and the only value she attached to his success was that it was his. Violent stimulus, he neither demanded nor received from her."[10] Indeed, Helen once told Margot Tennant, who was to be Asquith's second wife, that "after a weekend spent at Taplow with Lord and Lady Desborough ... though she, Helen, had enjoyed her visit, she did not think that she would ever care for the sort of society that I [Margot] loved, and was happier in the circle of her home and family."[11]

---

9   Ibid. i. 73.

10 Ibid. i. 45.

11 Margot Asquith, *Off the Record* (London: Frederick Muller, 1943), 11.

In her autobiography, Margot described her thus: "Henry's first wife, Helen Asquith, was an exceptionally pretty, refined woman; never dull, never artificial and of single-minded goodness. She had few illusions and was even less adventurous than her children."[12]

It is perhaps unsurprising that Asquith started an affair with Margot a few months before Helen's death. In the spring of 1891, he had dined at the House of Commons without Helen. Margot was there also as a guest. Thereafter, they saw each other constantly and started a regular exchange of long and intimate letters, even while Helen was still alive. Eventually, on 10 May 1894, he and Margot were married.[13]

Margot's background and temperament could not have been more different from Helen's. She had been born in 1864 in Scotland, one of twelve children, of whom four died. She wrote: "I remember nothing of my glorious youth except the violence of our family quarrels. Reckless waves of high and low spirits, added to quick tempers obliged my mother to separate us ... we raged and ragged until the small hours of the morning ... we were wild children and left to ourselves, had the time of our lives ... I was the most vital of the family and what the nurse described as a 'venturesome child'."[14] Characters are formed early in life, for better or worse, and change little thereafter. So it was with Margot.

She wrote: "There was a difference between the Tennants and the Asquiths ... Tennants believed in appealing to the hearts of men, firing their imagination and penetrating and vivifying their inmost lives ... we were as zealous and vital as they were detached and as cocky and passionate as they were modest and emotionless."[15] Asquith's son Herbert described her: "For Margot, with her vivid sense of the light

---

12 Margot Asquith, *Autobiography* (London: Thornton Butterworth Ltd., 1920), i. 284.

13 Ibid. 262.

14 Ibid. 18–19, 23.

15 Ibid. 269.

and colour of life, emotion was closely bound up with its expression. Daringly candid in writing and in speech, she was rarely hampered by a sense of reserve."[16]

Margot had had a somewhat frenetic love life, with many different lovers and constant changes of affection. Her father, Sir Charles Tennant, was one of the richest men in Britain. Margot's love affairs were in robust taste. They tended towards the hunting field. In succession they included Lord Rocksavage, Lord Ribblesdale (married to Margot's sister Charlotte, known as Charty), and Walter Long, MP. He too was married, but Margot's attitude, as it appeared in her diaries, was that conventional behaviour was not for her. She complained of the injustice of not being able to love a married man "even in private". She wrote: "Why should I appear indignant when I am kissed, or angry when fondled, its humbug when I like it.… Why should one only love one man, and he must be what we call right, not anyone else's husband, not even in private … why such an adjective as fast or flirt … it's sickening."[17]

Her affairs were legion. Alfred Lyttleton was one object of her affections, although it was to Laura that he directed his attentions, resulting in their getting married in May 1885. Lyttleton seems to have been something of a god. Tall, good-looking, and a sportsman of distinction who represented his country at cricket and football, he was also a real tennis champion for a number of years. Margot was madly in love with him. He was an aspiring politician, and a member of the bar. According to Margot, "he had everything at his feet … a man whose wholesome vitality and bounding life-spark knew nothing of illness or exhaustion, whose comprehensive intelligence and confident ambition defied defeat.… Everyone adored him. He combined the prowess at games of a good athlete with moral right-mindedness of a high order."[18] The death of her sister Laura after giving birth to a child caused Margot

---

16 Herbert Asquith, *Moments of Memory* (London: Hutchinson & Co., 1937), 90.

17 Margot Asquith, *Diary*, 3/1/98, 163 ff., 215.

18 Margot Asquith, *Autobiography* (London: Thornton Butterworth, London, 1920), i. 38.

deep grief and drew her closer to Lyttleton. She wrote: "I cling to you just now with passionate longing and complete happiness, for your directness of nature, your uncomplex morality, your star of success and healthy life-giving … be patient with me and don't condemn me if I don't immediately fulfil your hopes. Be tender if I turn to your sheltering arms and, if anything, give me a little more love just now at this parting of the ways." One author describes this as being "nothing more than the extravagant language of the times."[19]

Among others with whom she was associated were the poet Wilfred Blunt and Evan Charteris. Lyttleton was still a heartbreak for her, particularly when he remarried Margot's best friend, Edith (DD) Balfour. As she wrote in November 1891: "… perfect unions that might have been, do not come to pass … if Alfred had chosen me instead of Laura it might have been different."[20] Before she met Asquith there were two other affairs, one with Peter Flower and one with Arthur Milner.

Her affair with Peter Flower lasted for some nine years They had met at Ranelagh in the summer of 1883. She was aged 19 and fell instantly in love with him. He was many years older than her. He was something of a wastrel, running up debts and borrowing from friends, whom he did not repay. He had no visible means of support, though on one occasion he invested in a gold mine on a mineral reef in Mashonaland in South Africa. It came to nothing. Often ill-tempered and unreliable, he was a great womaniser. He treated Margot shabbily, but she always forgave him. They had a certain recklessness and love of excitement in common, but apart from hunting they had few mutual interests. She once said of him, "His power lies in lovemaking, not in loving."

There was still her affair with Milner. Arthur Milner was ten years older than Margot, and when they first met he was a fellow of Balliol College and a barrister. He was a favourite of Dr Jowett, Master of Balliol, and Margot was frequently invited to spend weekends at Balliol. Milner was a distinguished scholar who had won the Craven, Hertford,

---

19 Daphne Bennett, *Margot* (New York: Franklin Watts, 1985), 71–72.
20 Colin Clifford, *The Asquiths* (London: John Murray, 2002), 41–42.

Derby, and Eldon scholarships at Oxford. He achieved a first in Classics. He tried his hand at journalism and stood unsuccessfully as the Liberal candidate for Harrow at the general election in 1885. He had been appointed as private secretary to George Goschen, the chancellor of the exchequer.

Margot was charmed by Milner, and he for his part was in love with her. She managed to keep a relationship with both Milner and Flower at the same time, though they could not have been men more different in character. She wrote a number of gushing letters to Milner in her flamboyant style. She sent a lock of her hair and a book with a poem written by her. He dedicated his last book to her.

They were indeed unsuited to be married. He was deeply and seriously involved in his work, which was to take him to great prominence in the affairs of South Africa. For that he was created a viscount. He subsequently ended up in Lloyd George's Cabinet. But he lacked confidence and needed a woman who could give him constant reassurance that he was loved and needed, which Margot could never give him, although she was happy to play him along. Eventually, her meeting with Asquith put an end to her relations with Milner, to whom she wrote "I do not want you to learn anything of my affairs from the papers … but I want you to know that I am going to marry Asquith … You know me so well and what I dreamt of having but I *would never have found it* and this is the best I expect."[21]

Margot and Asquith had first met in 1890, but it was not until they sat next to each other at a dinner at the House of Commons in March 1891 that the affair blossomed. Helen died on 11 September 1891, by which time Asquith was writing to Margot every few days from the House of Commons and the Temple. She described the evening at the House of Commons. "When I first met Henry he knew nothing about me. We were sitting on the terrace of the House of Commons in the dark, continuing the conversation we had had throughout dinner … after a moment's silence he suddenly asked me what I was doing with

---

21 Ibid. i. 72–73.

my life; and I felt as if a gate had opened up in front of me.... we talked under the stars until a policeman informed us that the House was up. My new friendship was not only a great awakening for me, but a delight for my family and friends.... Asquith is the only kind of man that I could ever have married ... all the others are so much waste paper."[22] Asquith's reaction to meeting Margot was to tell her that "I have never been so fully happy as since I loved you. You have made me a different man.... better and stronger, I believe ... but certainly brighter and happier."[23]

The affair blew hot and cold. He told Frances Horner, with whom he also had an affair, that Margot did not love him as he loved her. Eventually, having given Peter Flower a farewell dinner, she and Asquith became engaged in February 1894, though she confided to her diary about "his lack of power of making love."[24] Five days after their wedding, on 10 May, she recorded in her diary, "I realised that in some ways with all his tact and delicacy, all his intellect and bigness, all his attributes, he had a commonplace side to him which nothing could alter ... it is not in his nature to feel the subtlety of love making, the dazzle and fun of it, the tiny almost untouchable fellowship of it ... He has passion, devotion, self-mastery, but not the nameless something that charms and compels and receives and combats a woman's most fastidious advances." Subsequently, after childbirth difficulties, she wrote, "I wished for him to sleep in his dressing room. He felt it all and knew by my change of manners instantly what had happened but I myself am incapable of measuring the depth of my own misery. I longed to die."[25]

Long before he met Margot, Asquith's legal career had taken off. After six or seven unproductive years at Fig Tree Court, he moved in 1883 to 1 Paper Buildings, the chambers of R.S. Wright (later Lord Wright). Their names still appear on the list of barristers on the board outside those chambers. Bowen's appointment to the High

---

22 Spender and Asquith, i. 97–98.
23 Clifford, 42.
24 Margot Asquith, *Diary*, 3/1/99.
25 Ibid.

Court Bench had left a vacancy for the position of Treasury Devil, and it was filled by A.L. Smith. In 1883, he too was promoted to the High Court Bench, and Wright was then nominated by the attorney general, Sir Henry James, QC (later Lord James of Hereford), to be the Treasury Devil. Asquith described Wright as the soundest classical scholar of his time (he too had been at Balliol) and "one of the best hearted and most generous of men."[26] From being Wright's "devil",[27] Asquith gradually acquired work of his own, so that by 1885 he had the makings of a substantial and growing practice which included work for the attorney general himself.

Three particular assignments had important consequences for Asquith. The first related to the Bradlaugh case. Bradlaugh was elected as a Member of Parliament for Northampton in 1880, but as a radical atheist, he refused to take the parliamentary oath. This resulted in his not being allowed to take his seat, whereupon the electors re-elected him, to the considerable embarrassment of the Gladstone administration. In 1886, the government decided to introduce an affirmation bill to resolve the problem, and Asquith found himself preparing a detailed memorandum for the prime minister on the theory and practice of the parliamentary oath. The attorney general had sent the instructions to Wright, who passed them on to Asquith. His well-drafted memorandum received approval from both the attorney and the prime minister. Bradlaugh was eventually allowed to take the oath in 1886, and in 1888 an oaths act, allowing, affirmation was passed.

Asquith's second important assignment arose in 1883, when the attorney introduced the Corrupt Practices Act, which Asquith helped to draft. It related primarily to the conduct of elections. As a result, he was invited by the attorney to prepare a short manual, to guide election agents and others through the intricacies of the new legislation. Asquith produced a small book, *An Election Guide – rules*

---

26 Earl of Oxford and Asquith, *Memories and Reflections* (London: Cassell and Company, Ltd., 1928), 82.

27 A *devil* is a barrister who drafts documents and advises a more senior barrister about the briefs sent to the latter.

for the conduct of elections in England and Wales under the Corrupt Practices Act 1883. It was published in 1884 by the Liberal Central Association. It had two consequences. It brought Asquith close to leading figures in the Liberal party, and after the general election in 1885, it resulted in increased work for him at the bar. After an election, an unsuccessful candidate may petition the courts to set aside the result because of some alleged irregularity perpetrated by his opponent. As an expert in the new electoral system, Asquith was in great demand as junior counsel by many of the Liberal candidates involved in election petitions.

Ireland had been a problem for the government throughout this period, and Gladstone recognised that the only way to try and pacify Ireland was to grant home rule to the Irish. In April 1886, he introduced what was to be his first home rule bill. In June, on its second reading, it was defeated, 343 votes to 313. Ninety-three MPs who had been elected as Liberals voted against Gladstone, including (most importantly) Joseph Chamberlain and the Marquis of Hartington. Gladstone recommended an immediate dissolution. In the ensuing general election, Asquith was elected as MP for East Fife with a modest majority of 385, but the Conservatives under Lord Salisbury won the majority of seats.

In 1888, Asquith came into further prominence as junior counsel to Sir Charles Russell, QC, (later Lord Russell of Killowen) in the Parnell inquiry. Parnell was a leader of the Irish Nationalist party and had transformed the Irish Parliamentary Party into a formidable and highly disciplined machine. In April 1887, the *Times* published a facsimile copy of five letters purporting to be signed by Parnell, which were allegedly addressed to Patrick Egan, a notorious Irish dynamiter. There were also six letters purporting to have been written by Egan himself. They suggested that Parnell was complicit in Irish terrorism. One letter, allegedly written by Parnell, relating to the murders in Phoenix Park of Lord Cavendish and Frederick Burke, an undersecretary in the Dublin Castle Administration, read:

"15/5/82

Dear Sir,

I am not surprised at your friend's anger, but he and you should know that to denounce the murders was the only course open to us. To do so promptly was plainly our best policy. But you can tell him [Egan] and all the others concerned, that though I regret the accident of Lord F. Cavendish's death, I cannot refuse to admit that Burke got no more than his deserts. You are at liberty to show him this, and others whom you can trust also, but let not my address be known. He can write to the House of Commons.

Yours very truly

Chas. S. Parnell"

Parnell alleged that it was a forgery but declined to proceed in the English Courts. Instead, he asked for an independent select parliamentary committee to be set up to enquire into the authenticity (or otherwise) of the allegations. The Conservative government refused and appointed three judges with known Union sympathies to enquire as a commission, not merely into the authenticity of the letters, but also into the other allegations by the *Times* concerning the criminal behaviour of the Irish. Asquith was instructed on behalf of Parnell, being led by Russell.

The inquiry lasted for many months and ranged over the whole course of recent Irish history. This was because the commission sought to postpone argument about the authenticity of the letters until they had investigated (at interminable length) the allegations of terrorism against the Irish. They hoped that the latter would perhaps thereby conceal the government's difficulties over the letters.

Eventually, the commission did turn to the letters. Russell cross-examined Pigott, who had forged the letters and given them to the *Times*. Russell destroyed him. Before he had fully completed his evidence, Pigott fled to Paris and then to Madrid, where he shot himself. However, Russell's cross-examination of Soames of the *Times*, who had been involved in the negotiations for the letters, was less successful. The manager of the *Times*, C.J. Macdonald, was also called to give evidence to explain how it happened that the *Times* had come to accept the letters in the first place, and why they chose to publish them thereafter, apparently without taking any steps to check their authenticity.

Macdonald had had no part in the negotiations with Pigott, which had been conducted by a man called Houston. Macdonald made a poor showing in the witness box. The *Times* described him in this way: "Macdonald, at this time was 67 and feeling the effect of his age. The business, arising out of the preparation for the Commission itself, had placed a specially heavy burden on his shoulders and there were signs that his strength was beginning to break down under the strain. He had in fact only a few months to live.... in the months preceding the meeting of the Commission, he had definitely lost control of the business of the department ... his letters from 1887 onwards, are few, halting and sometimes despondent."[28]

In one of his memoirs, Asquith himself gave a graphic picture of what happened after the close of Macdonald's examination-in-chief: "As he [Macdonald] was one of the principal witnesses, it would, of course, naturally have fallen to Russell to cross-examine him; and I was never more surprised in my life than when, just as the Court rose for lunch, he turned to me and said 'I am tired: you must take charge of this fellow.' I protested, but in vain, and I was left to the critical task of conducting the cross-examination; a task made all the more formidable, because my leader, the greatest cross-examiner at the English Bar, sat there throughout and listened. I got on to what proved to be an effective, and, even, a destructive line of attack, and in the course of a couple of hours, made the largest step in advance that I ever took in my forensic career."[29]

---

28 *History of the Times*, iii. 69.

29 *Memories*, 79–80.

Some flavour of the cross-examination can be gathered from the following.

> Q: "Did Houston say that he had paid £1,780 for these eleven letters? *Yes.*
>
> Q: Did he not tell you, to whom? *No.*
>
> Q: Or how? *No.*
>
> Q: Or when? *No.*
>
> Q: Or where? *No.*
>
> Q: Showed you no voucher or receipt? *None whatsoever.*
>
> Q: No particulars, whether in items or a lump sum? *No.*
>
> Q: Did he represent to you that he was ready to let the *Times* have the letters for publication on being recouped? *Yes.*
>
> Q: Nothing more? *No.*
>
> Q: And you have not, as I understand, up to this moment investigated the details of Mr Houston's alleged expenditure? *I have not.*
>
> Q: You have taken his word for it throughout? *I have.*"[30]

This was not to be the last time the paper was seriously at fault in checking its sources. There are faint echoes in the story of the *Hitler Diaries* and Lord Dacre, though the sources of the information there were quite different.

---

30   *History of the Times*, iii 77.

Asquith's cross-examination was undoubtedly a tour de force, and Russell overwhelmed him with the generosity of his praises and congratulations. The reputation of the *Times* was severely damaged. Both it and Macdonald had to make a grovelling apology.

Asquith's practice now grew substantially. Shortly afterwards, at the age of 37, he "took silk". To take silk means that a barrister is appointed a QC by the Lord Chancellor, which is an honour, and involves more prestigious and more lucrative work. His services were in great demand by railway companies and county councils. This was the result of the passing in 1888 of the Railway and Canal Traffic Act and of the Local Government Act.

Among his other cases that attracted public interest was the case of Carlill v Carbolic Smoke Ball Company, in which he appeared in the trial before Mr Justice Hawkins as leading counsel for the defendants.

The headnote in the *Law Report* reads:

> "The defendants who were the proprietors and vendors of a medical preparation called "The Carbolic Smoke Ball" inserted in the *Pall Mall Gazette* of 13 November 1891 the following advertisement "100*l* reward will be paid by the Carbolic Smoke Ball Company to any person who contracts the increasing epidemic influenza colds, or any disease by taking cold, after having used the ball three times daily, for two weeks, according to the printed directions supplied with each ball. 1000*l* is deposited with the Alliance Bank, Regent Street, showing our sincerity in the matter. During the last epidemic of influenza, many thousand carbolic smoke balls were sold as preventatives against this disease, and in no ascertained case was the disease contracted by those using the carbolic smoke ball. One carbolic smoke ball will last a family several months, making it the cheapest remedy in the world at the price, 10s post free.

The ball can be refilled at a cost of 5s. Address; Carbolic Smoke Ball Company, 27, Princes Street, Hanover Square, London, W."

The head note continued:

"The plaintiff, a lady, having read that advertisement, on the faith of it, bought one of the defendants' carbolic smoke balls, and used it as directed three times a day, from 20 November till 17 January, 1892, when she was attacked by influenza. She thereupon brought this action against the defendants to recover the 100*l* promised in their advertisement.[31]

Many and varied were the ingenious arguments put forward by Asquith on behalf of the defendants. (1) There was no contract. (2) If there were a contract, wholly or partly in writing, it required a stamp. (3) It was in any event a wagering contract. (4) It was a contract of insurance.

The judge laid down important principles of contract law. The advertisement amounted to a general promise or contract to pay the offered sum to any person who performed the condition mentioned in it. The other submissions were also dismissed. When the defendants appealed, Asquith was no longer briefed and the court of appeal dismissed their appeal. They said that the contention that this was an insurance policy or a bet was not worth serious consideration and that the offer was not a "puff" or "mere waste paper".[32]

Asquith had also been engaged as counsel in a case of considerable more interest to the gossip-minded public in what came to be called the "Royal Baccarat Scandal" in June 1891. This was not only a matter of interest to the general public involving the Prince of Wales in a betting scandal, but served to enhance Asquith's reputation as a skilful

---

31 !892, 2.QB, 484–485.

32 QB 1893, i. 256–275.

advocate. Although he had by this time been a QC for some years, he was again led by Russell on behalf of the defendants. The case of Gordon-Cumming v Wilson and Others arose from events which occurred between 8 September and 10 September 1890 at Tranby Croft, the country home of shipbuilder Sir Arthur Wilson. There was a big house party. Some of the guests had been at Doncaster Races, one of them the Prince of Wales. During the first evening, some of the guests played baccarat, a card game that involves gambling – illegal in England. Colonel Sir William Gordon-Cumming, Bart, was observed by some of the other guests apparently cheating by altering the amount of the bets which he had put on the table after he had won or lost a hand. On the second evening, some guests, now alerted to Gordon-Cumming's conduct, watched him more closely. Their previous suspicions were confirmed. In the course of the two evenings, Gordon-Cumming had won a total of £228. Next morning, six of the guests conferred about what to do about his behaviour. They challenged him. He denied any wrongdoing. His challengers decided that the matter should be reported to Lord Coventry and General Owan Williams, who were also house guests. Under some pressure from Williams and Coventry, Gordon-Cumming signed a pledge never to play card games again in exchange for an agreement that the matter would remain secret. It turned out to be a fatal error. He continued, however, to maintain his innocence. The matter did not remain secret for long. It was thought that Daisy, Lady Brooke, the Prince of Wales' mistress, was responsible for its circulation. It was soon the talk of society. Gordon-Cumming found himself ostracised. In order to defend his reputation, he decided to bring proceedings for slander against the guests who had made the accusations against him. Russell was responsible for cross-examining the plaintiff and the Prince of Wales as well as examining-in-chief some of the defendants. Asquith's task was to cross examine Williams, who had been responsible for Gordon-Cumming signing the pledge, and to examine-in-chief two of the guests, Arthur Wilson (Sir Arthur's son) and his brother-in-law Lycett Green. Both had observed Gordon-Cumming's behaviour.

Wilson told the court what he had observed on the first evening. "He [Gordon-Cumming] drew a very bad card ... immediately he saw this, he drew back his hands to his own pile ... and let fall counters ... into his own pile." In answer to Asquith's further question: "Did you say anything to Mr Berkeley Levett (next to whom the witness was sitting)?" Wilson replied, "Yes, directly I saw this, I turned round to him and whispered, 'My God, Berkeley, this is too hot....' Mr Levett said, 'What on earth do you mean?' I said, 'This man next to me is cheating.' Levett said, 'My dear chap, you must be mistaken – it is absolutely impossible.' I said to him, 'Well just look for yourself.' He looked, and a few coups later Levett turned to me and said, 'It is too hot'."

Asquith asked, "After the game was over, did you go to Mr Levett's room?"

"Yes." There, Levett said. "My God! To think of it – Lieutenant Colonel Sir William Gordon-Cumming, Bart, cheating at cards!"[33]

After similar behaviour was observed on the second evening, they decided that the matter should be reported to Coventry, who was one of their longest friends and one of the oldest members of the party. Williams was also consulted. In due course, they decided that the matter had to be reported to the Prince of Wales. The evidence given by Lycett Green in answer to Asquith's questions was intended to support that of Wilson, but when he was cross-examined by Charles Gill, QC, for Gordon-Cumming, he made a poor showing.[34]

However, it was Asquith's cross-examination of Williams about the plaintiff signing the undertaking not to play cards again that played a decisive part in the determination of the case. The undertaking read: "In consideration of the promise made by the gentlemen whose names are subscribed, to preserve silence with reference to an accusation which has been made in regard to my conduct at baccarat, on the nights of Monday and Tuesday, the 8th and 9th September, 1890, at

---

33 W. Teignmouth Shore, *The Baccarat Case* (Edinburgh and London: William Hodge & Company Ltd., 1932), 115–116.

34 Rt. Hon. Sir Michael Havers, QC, MP and Edward Grayson, *The Royal Baccarat Scandal*, 2nd edition (Souvenir Press Ltd., 1988), 153–154.

Tranby Croft, I will, on my part, solemnly undertake never to play cards again, as long as I live. [Signed] W. Gordon-Cumming." Ten names were subscribed.

Asquith continued to question Williams.

> Q: "Do you remember at that interview [between Gordon-Cumming and the Prince of Wales] any reference being made to the Duke of Cambridge and his commanding officer?
>
> A: … I felt that we had gone a long way out of our way to deal leniently with him [Gordon-Cumming] and I said, "You are at perfect liberty to refer the matter to the Duke of Cambridge or your Commanding Officer, but I can assure you that neither one nor the other will likely deal so leniently in the matter as Lord Coventry and myself."
>
> Q: I understand you to say that Sir William Gordon-Cumming said that a signature to the paper was tantamount to an admission of his guilt. You and Lord Coventry assented?
>
> A. Yes, we did.
>
> Q. You said it would be such an acknowledgement?
>
> A. Undoubtedly.…
>
> Q: You assert you told him it was the only way out of the impasse?
>
> A: We certainly advised him to sign it. We maintained that unless he signed it, he would be requested to leave the house the following morning, and proclaimed over every racecourse as a cheat.…

Q: Do you conceive that in the advice which you gave, and in your whole dealing with this matter, that you were acting in his interest as an old friend?

A: I do."[35]

Asquith's cross-examination was favourably commented on by a distinguished lawyer many years later. "Asquith's methods, though less spectacular than Russell's, were not ineffectual. He insisted at some length on the General's friendship for Gordon-Cumming, to imply that such a close friend would never have believed the charges against him unless he had found the evidence overwhelming … to imply also that the General had been thrown into a state of terrible shock, not at the prospect of the Prince (and himself) being involved in a scandal, but because his friend had been accused of cheating … it had to be gradually insinuated and it took many words and bored the audience who were looking for sensations."[36]

The trial lasted from 1 June until 9 June, when the jury retired. They deliberated for only ten minutes and returned a verdict in favour of the defendants. Gordon-Cumming was dismissed from the army and retired in disgrace to his Scottish estate, still maintaining his innocence.

While from a very slow start Asquith's legal career had only gradually taken off, his political career, on the other hand, was a success almost from the beginning. He experienced a meteoric rise through the political ranks. He had been in the House of Commons for no more than six years and had made few speeches there, so that it occasioned some surprise when, on Salisbury's resignation in June 1892, Gladstone appointed Asquith to be his home secretary. While his maiden speech in March 1887, on the topic of the Irish Crimes Bill, had been greeted by Chamberlain with a friendly compliment, Asquith had hitherto held no office of any kind and had spent his whole time as an MP on the

---

35   Ibid. 90–93.

36   Havers, 115.

back benches. He was just under 40 and the youngest member of the Cabinet. Eight of his colleagues were well over 60. Of the rest, only two were under 54. In 1892, Gladstone himself was aged 83.

Asquith's tenure of the Home Office proved a success. One of the many measures he introduced was to deal with the problems of public meetings in Trafalgar Square. A total ban imposed by the previous home secretary was replaced by a right to hold meetings during daylight on weekends, provided notice to the police was given in advance. Such regulations are not dissimilar to those that obtain today. He was also much involved in the preparation of the Disestablishment of the Welsh Churches Bill. Asquith was also asked to speak on another of Gladstone's home rule bills, but his was not a major contribution. Its defeat by the House of Lords on its second reading finally led to Gladstone's resignation in March 1894. He was replaced by Lord Rosebery. The Liberal Government, with Asquith still as Home Secretary, lingered on until Rosebery resigned in June 1895.

Asquith's main contribution at the Home Office was to introduce an important factories act, designed to promote the health and safety of factory workers. At the general election in 1895, the Liberals were routed, but Asquith retained his seat. He thereupon returned to a successful private practice at the bar.

The Conservatives remained in power, first under Salisbury, and then under Balfour, from 1902 until December 1905, when he resigned. The overwhelming Liberal victory in the 1906 general election was to usher in one of the most distinguished governments of all time. But before it took office, there was to be high political drama and intrigue. Campbell-Bannerman had succeeded Rosebery as Liberal leader. However, he was perceived as being incapable of holding his own against the experienced Conservatives on the opposition bench. There was a suggestion from colleagues that he should go to the House of Lords and leave the conduct of affairs in the House of Commons to one of them. This idea resulted in the so-called "Regulas Compact" in September 1905. Its name was taken from a fishing lodge in Morayshire, near where Asquith, Grey, and Haldane (leading Liberals) all happened to be. The arrangement made between them was that they should decline to take office in a Campbell-Bannerman administration unless he went to the House of Lords. This would leave Asquith as leader of the House of Commons and chancellor of the exchequer, Grey would be foreign or colonial secretary, and Haldane, the lord chancellor.

It was Asquith's responsibility to persuade Campbell-Bannerman of the good sense of the Compact. Haldane was deputed to get the approval of the King, whose constitutional position was to ensure that the prime minister was able to hold down the burden of being both prime minister and leader of the House of Commons. Asquith professed to believe that there was nothing unedifying in these transactions nor was there anything in the nature of an intrigue.[37]

Margot's record of what happened at the meeting between Asquith and Campbell-Bannerman on 13 November does not indicate any sort of pressure by Asquith to force Campbell-Bannerman to go to the Lords.

> "Henry told me that he had seen Sir Henry Campbell-Bannerman…. he [Campbell-Bannerman] said that things looked like they were coming to a head politically, and that any day after Parliament met, we might expect a General election. C.B. gathered that he [C.B] would probably be the man the King would send for …
>
> Henry said, "C.B. then looked at me and said 'I do not think we have ever spoken of the future Liberal Government, Asquith? What would you like? The Exchequer I suppose?' … I said nothing … 'or the Home Office?' said C.B "I said certainly not. At which he [C.B.] said, 'Of course, if you want legal promotion, what about the Woolsack? [i.e. Lord Chancellor] No? Well then", said C.B " it comes back to the Exchequer. I hear it has been suggested by that ingenious person,

---

37 *Memoirs*, 194–196.

Richard Burdon Haldane, that I should go to the House of Lords, a place for which I have neither liking, training nor ambition."

Margot went on:

"I could see that the impression left upon Henry's mind, while he was telling me of this conversation, was that it would be with reluctance, and even repugnance, that Campbell-Bannerman would ever go to the House of Lords."[38]

In further conversation, Asquith pressed for Grey to go to the Foreign Office and Haldane to get the Woolsack.

By December, Asquith had changed his position. He foresaw serious difficulties in the formation of a new government without the three leading members in it. He convinced himself that he could not stand aside. He was now willing to join the Government, even if Campbell-Bannerman remained in the House of Commons. When he was formally offered the exchequer, he accepted. Grey took a different view and told Campbell-Bannerman that unless he went to the Lords, he (Grey) would not accept office. Eventually, after a good deal of anguished deliberation, he too eventually accepted the Foreign Office. Haldane, meanwhile, had been offered the War Office, which he accepted. He was to make a major contribution to the efficiency of the army, to which Field Marshal Haig paid handsome tribute at the end of the war.[39] Sir Robert Reid became lord chancellor with the title of Lord Loreburn.

On 5 December, Campbell-Bannerman had been to see the King to kiss hands. Traditionally, when a minister is appointed it is customary for him or her actually to kiss the Sovereign's hand. Margot's diary

---

38 Margot Asquith, *Autobiography*, ii 66–68.

39 On 19 April 1919, after taking part in the Peace Parade, Haig, who had commanded the successful British Army in France, called at Haldane's house in the evening and presented him with a copy of his *War Despatches* on which he had inscribed "To the Greatest Secretary of State of War England has ever had."

suggests that though the King invited Campbell-Bannerman to form a government, the actual kissing of hands did not take place. More importantly, the King pointed out to Campbell-Bannerman that he was no longer as young as he used to be and suggested that he should go to the Lords. Campbell-Bannerman answered "that no doubt he would ultimately be obliged to do this, but he would prefer starting in the Commons if only for a short time."[40] The general election, which followed in January, resulted in an overwhelming victory for the Liberals with a majority of some 350 seats.

The new government carried out a whole series of reforms, which were to transform the political map. There were proposals to restore self-government to the Transvaal, to reverse the decision in the Taff Vale judgement (which by the Trade Disputes Act had made trade unions liable for damages), and to revoke the provisions of the Education Act introduced by the Conservatives in 1902. This act had allocated government funds to church and Catholic schools. However, the House of Lords, with its inbuilt Conservative majority, emasculated this Liberal bill in committee, and it was dropped. This was the first shot fired in what was to be a titanic struggle between the Liberals and the House of Lords and was to occupy the political arena until the passing of the Parliament Act in 1911. A start was made to the provision of old age pensions, insurance schemes, and differential tax rates. These were social reforms, which were the forerunner of the modern welfare state.

In November 1907, Campbell-Bannerman suffered a severe heart attack, and although he returned to the House of Commons to speak on 12 February 1908, he then suffered another heart attack. It was not until 3 April 1908 that he wrote to the King, offering his resignation. As a result, Asquith became prime minister.

The two major political issues which divided the country between 1908 and the outbreak of war in August 1914 were the attempts by the Liberals to reduce the obstruction of the House of Lords, and to find a permanent solution to the Irish problem. How to deal with the

---

40   Margot Asquith, *Autobiography*, ii. 72.

intransigence of the Lords fully occupied the minds of the Liberal leaders. The rejection of their Licensing Bill of 1908 was merely one example, which confirmed Asquith and his colleagues in their view of the necessity of seeking ways to prevent the House of Lords from obstructing legislation to which the elected government subscribed. A suggestion that the Commons should pass so many measures as to swamp the Lords was sensibly rejected. It was decided that bills should be chosen in such a way as to acquire political capital in the event of their rejection by the Lords. Money bills were selected as the vehicle to achieve this objective.

In 1909, the naval estimates caused something of a furore. It was the age-old conflict between the treasury and the armed forces, this time over the number of new dreadnought battleships to be built. There was a demand for six by the Admiralty, while the treasury favoured only four. The cry went up: "We want eight and we won't wait." In the result there was a typical English compromise by which four were to be built immediately and four more when the necessity arose.

The effect of this expenditure, which was not universally popular, as well as the cost of the old age pensions, meant that the government, in addition to having to introduce a radical budget in any event, was now constrained somehow to raise substantial extra revenue by way of increased taxes. This gave rise to Lloyd George's famous budget of 1909, in which land taxes and super taxes were the most controversial measures. When the peers rejected the finance bill, Asquith sought and obtained an immediate dissolution, which resulted in the return of the Liberal government, but with a much reduced majority. They were thereafter dependant on the support of the Irish Nationalists. The idea of persuading the King to agree to create further peers, to ensure that the Lords were no longer able to thwart the will of the Commons, fell into abeyance when Edward VII died and was succeeded by George V.

Eventually, the new King agreed that if the Liberals won the next general election, he would use his prerogative to create more peers. The Liberals again won and set about introducing measures to control the power of the peers. On 10 August 1911, the House of Lords finally passed the Parliament Bill. This limited the power of the peers to obstruct government business. Thereafter, a whole series of industrial disputes, in addition to the suffragette campaign, occupied the government, but it was Ireland which was to hold the centre stage in the political arena in the years leading up to 4 August 1914. While these difficult political problems occupied Asquith, his private life took a very different turn.

Venetia

CHAPTER THREE

Venetia

Venetia's relationship with Asquith arose indirectly out of a fatal accident suffered in December 1909 by Archie Gordon, son of Lord and Lady Aberdeen. He was the boyfriend of Asquith's daughter Violet. Venetia and Violet had been very close friends from their early teens, and Venetia was a frequent visitor to Downing Street. She was the daughter of Lord Sheffield, the 4th Baron, who was sometimes known as Lord Stanley of Alderley. She was born in 1887 and lived until 1948. The Stanley family had been connected with Alderley, Cheshire, since the fifteenth century and owned Alderley Park. Their town house in London was 18 Mansfield Street, W.1 and they had a country estate at Penrhos, on the Anglesey coast near Holyhead. Cynthia Asquith (who was married to Asquith's second son, Beb) recorded a conversation in which Margot expressed the view that Venetia was not Lord Sheffield's child.[41] In fact, Venetia is believed to have been the daughter of the 9th Earl of Carlisle, with whom her mother had had an affair.[42]

In November 1904, Violet was in Paris. She had been sent there to accompany her brother Oc, who was to learn French as a precursor to a life in the city. Venetia visited them both while they were there. Thereafter, they were part of the same social set. Some idea of the social life they led is to found in Violet's diary for August 1907. "I shalln't say

---

41   Lady Cynthia Asquith, *Lady Cynthia Asquith Diaries, 1915–1918* (Hutchinson & Co., 1968), 283.

42   Clifford, 409 n.

a word about the end of the season – it tires me to think of it. My last week, I had 5 balls running and Raymond's [her brother's] wedding.... When it was all over I lay down.... There was still the ball to face.... I minded it acutely at first... but began to feel quite happy after dancing an 8 some reel.... It lasted till 4.30!"[43]

Violet and Venetia used to meet frequently in London, Scotland, Gloucestershire, Anglesey, Alderley, and elsewhere. They wrote gushing girlie letters to each other. In October 1906, Violet was writing to Venetia "Dearest Venetia – I would love to come to Alderley on the 11th Dec – what fun it will be – do – do lets have the Morris dance for hours and hours.... write at once and say you are glad I am coming...."[44]

In July 1907, Violet wrote to Venetia, "Goodbye Darling – I wish you weren't gone ... Write to me very often and don't stop loving me."[45] Venetia replied in much the same fashion, addressing her as "my Darling" and ending "Goodbye ever dearest".

Violet recognised what a true friend Venetia was when in May 1908 she wrote, "My darling Only one line to say the joy and help you have been to me in these 2 strangest of strange weeks. Living has felt like dreaming ... & a thick veil seems to hang between me and what have always been the realest and clearest things – (I mean things like my relations with people I know as well as my carpet).... You have been my one firm footing all through. Bless you."[46]

In October, Violet was writing, "My very Dearest – Don't be angry with me – this is nearly my first letter since I saw you last.... Write at once darling to Yr V. Burn this letter because of vulgar allusions to various navigations."[47]

---

43 Mark Bonham Carter and Mark Pottle, eds., *Lantern Slides: The Diaries and Letters of Violet Bonham Carter 1904–1914* (London: Weidenfeld and Nicolson, 1996), 134.

44 Ibid. 112.

45 Ibid. 133.

46 Ibid. 158.

47 Ibid. 165.

Archie Gordon, Lord Aberdeen's son, had been an admirer of Violet for some time. In November 1909, he was in a horrendous motor accident. Although he lived for another twenty days, he died from his injuries in Winchester Hospital on 16 December. Violet was at his bedside for the last hours, and they announced an engagement. Accompanying her was Venetia, whose visit Violet described in her Diary: "Venetia came up which made him very happy." She then recorded Gordon's conversation with Venetia: "'What did the people at Mansfield Street [Venetia's home] say to <u>this</u>?' he asked … then to me, 'Venetia will have to nearly live with us, won't she? … then Gordon added 'kiss me, Venetia." She went away and he seemed very tired.'"[48]

In 1910, Violet and Venetia were on holiday together in France and continued thereafter to meet and exchange letters. One correspondent wrote to Violet, "Dear child, I only told Venetia about the watch. I thought she knew all your tenderest secrets."[49]

The earliest extant letter from Asquith to Venetia is dated 10 September 1910. Thereafter, correspondence was sporadic until 1912. In April 1911, Asquith was very ill at home, complaining of feeling giddy. Because it was Budget Day, Margot got him downstairs in Downing Street but made sure he cried off the budget dinner to be held in the House of Commons. She arranged for the doctor to call in the evening because she was going to a concert. When she returned later that night, she expected to find her ailing husband in the house. When he finally returned, it transpired that he had spent the evening in the Cabinet room, writing to Venetia.[50]

Their affair appears to have started in earnest in January 1912, when Venetia and Violet spent a holiday in Sicily with Asquith and Montagu, who was Asquith's private secretary. It seems to have been something of a rather jolly romp. Violet recorded: "We played hiding in the garden & jumping out after dark. Montagu is the best person in the world to play

---

48   Ibid. 193.

49   Ibid. 278.

50   Clifford, 192.

it with. He is <u>so</u> frightened – and <u>so</u> frightening."[51] Not long after this holiday, Venetia went to stay with Asquith for the weekend at a house lent to him by a cousin in the New Forest.

On 1 April 1912, he was able to write to her in these terms:

> "Dearest Venetia – I want to see you (& *must*) before you go and I hear from Violet that you might be able to come here (H of C) tomorrow (Tuesday) to hear the Budget; in any case after it, at tea time in my room – you will come, won't you?
>
> – Ever yr loving
>
> HHA"

At this time, Venetia was 24. She had been privately educated by tutors and governesses, and it is clear from Asquith's letters that she was an intelligent and well read girl, with a good knowledge of English literature and much interested in politics. She was also an avid birdwatcher. Cynthia Asquith described her as "very, very nice".[52] Venetia's family were staunchly liberal and she was a first cousin of Clementine Churchill. Pictures of her at the time show her dark-haired, dark-eyed, lively and, though no beauty, not unattractive, although Violet subsequently told Jenkins that "Venetia was so plain".[53]

She has been variously described. "An exciting, brilliant, liberated woman … years ahead of her time. An attractive woman, but far from a stunning one … with intelligence, excitement, force of personality and political sophistication."[54] Asquith once described her as a "Blue

---

51 *Lantern Slides* 297.

52 Cynthia Asquith, 17.

53 *Lantern Slides*, xxviii.

54 Naomi B. Levine, *Politics, Religion and Love* (New York: New York University Press, 1991), xii. 1, 102.

Stocking".[55] Elsewhere she was described as "Tall, strongly built, formidably intelligent, she was lacking in seductive charm. She had the reputation of rendering even the most virile man impotent."[56] In the light of her association with a number of lovers, this latter description may not be entirely accurate.

Her friend Sir Laurence Jones left this picture of her in her youth: "She was a splendid, virginal, comradely creature, reserving for herself for we knew not what use of her fine brain and hidden heart."[57] Others had a different view. Margot once described Venetia in a letter she wrote to Montagu in March, 1914. "If Venetia had an ounce of truth and candour ... I should smile, but she is even teaching Henry to avoid telling me things.... A woman without refinement or any imagination whatever.... How I loathe girls who can't love but claim and collect like a cuckoo for their own vanity. Venetia's head is completely turned."[58] On 16 April 1915, she wrote to Montagu, "She [Venetia] is not *candid* with me. She has not much atmosphere of moral or intellectual sensibility." Given Margot's well-known proclivity for exaggeration and her obvious feeling of jealousy, this view of Venetia can perhaps be taken with a slight pinch of salt. Montagu, who was Asquith's private secretary, and who subsequently married Venetia, described her as "terrifyingly selfless".[59]

In May 1910, when they were both staying with the Aberdeens at the Vice Regal Lodge in Dublin, Violet described Venetia. "She [Venetia] was a transformed being here! very painstaking, feminine, bright and avenante ... her gruff baritone changed to a siren soprano ... shooting glittering glances hither and thither ... wearing a new 'fish' every night & spending tete a tete days at the Zoo with the A.D.C's.! A Vice-Regal Court is certainly her assiette ... & bogus captains her element! (all

---

55 Herbert Henry Asquith, *Letters from Lord Oxford to a Friend 1922-1927* (London: Geoffrey Bles, 1934), 18.

56 Philip Ziegler, *Diana Cooper* (Harmondsworth: Penguin Books, 1983), 74.

57 Laurence Jones, *An Edwardian Youth* (Macmillan & Co., 1956), 214.

58 Montagu, MSS.

59 Cynthia Asquith, 73.

the A.D.C's here are called captain though civilians) – they are mostly bounders of the deepest dye ... It is sad to think how much time she has wasted in the wrong place!!"[60]

In the years before the outbreak of the war, she was one of the leading members of a group who came to be known as the Corrupt Coterie. It was composed of the children of The Souls, a remarkable group of friends who were very intelligent, articulate people who happened to share a love of good talk. They were intellectuals: questioning, sceptical, and philosophical. According to some, they prided themselves on their spirituality,[61] though not all members such as Keynes, Strachey, or Moore could be so described. The group had started its existence in July 1889 as a result of a dinner given by George Curzon at his club for a group of his closest friends. They were mostly aristocratic, though nobility was not a precondition – wit was. They believed "that they were moving away from philistinism, towards patronage of the arts; away from political divisions – towards greater tolerance on political matters ... above all they believed they were restoring to the English upper classes, an art they had almost lost, the art of intelligent conversation."[62]

Their children had known each other since childhood and were automatically born into the Coterie. They included, inter alios, apart from Venetia, Raymond Asquith, who had had an academic record equal to his father's. He had been a scholar at Winchester and Balliol. He had won the Craven, Ireland, and Derby Scholarships, got a first in Greats and was a fellow of All Souls. Older than the others, he was regarded as their leader. Diana Manners (later Diana Cooper) wrote: "Yet of all of them he was the most disciplined and loved. Everything he taught me by example became direction through my life."[63] He had a successful practice at the bar and was adopted as Liberal candidate for

---

60 *Lantern Slides*, 207.

61 Philip Ziegler, *Diana Cooper* (London: Penguin Books, 1983), 45.

62 Angela Lambert, *Unquiet Souls* (London: Macmillan, 1984), 32.

63 Diana Cooper, *The Rainbow Comes and Goes* (London: Rupert Hart-Davis, 1958), 99.

Derby, but his political career never had time to mature. He concealed his academic abilities behind a facade of pleasure-seeking and a caustic wit. His father thought that "he was rarely endowed but needed a goad or spark." His reserve was sometimes misread for inhumanity, and his letter to his brother Cyril, who had also won the first Balliol scholarship, speaks volumes about his character. "DEAR CYRIL Fancy *you* being as clever as … Raymond."[64]

Hugo (Ego) and Ivo Charteris were members. The former became honorary attaché in Washington in 1908. He was described as "the nearest to a knight of chivalry – while his humour was a riot of fine flowers and herbs. No one had such flavour, or such humility and philosophy."[65] In 1905, Violet described him as "utterly devoid of a sense of humour or responsiveness of any kind",[66] but a few months later wrote, "I never misjudged anyone more than Ego. He is most delightful & made very good remarks with that vacant expression never-varying, which discouraged me at first."[67] Almost all the members volunteered to join the army. Their attitude was summed up by Rupert Brooke (himself to die at Gallipoli):

> "Now God be thanked who has matched us with His hour
> And caught our youth, and waken'd us from sleeping."

Billy and Julian Grenfell had both been to Eton and Balliol and were contemporaries of Cyril Asquith. They were the sons of the 1st Baron Desborough. Julian was the author of a famous poem: "Into Battle". He wrote home from the Western Front that it was the best fun one could dream about, like a picnic without the objectlessness of a picnic. He enjoyed war because there was a sincerity and truth to war that he had not found elsewhere.[68] But, Diana thought there was a brutal

---

64 *Spender*, ii. 222.

65 *Cooper*, 79a.

66 *Lantern Slides*, 63.

67 Ibid. 93.

68 Nicholas Moseley, *Julian Grenfell* (London: 1976).

heartiness, an insensitivity about the Grenfells which accorded ill with the decadence that was her favoured affectation. She did not actively disapprove of their anti-Semitism, their crude consciousness of caste, or their worship of the traditional manly qualities, but there was a stridency, a vulgarity about them that she deplored. She found a little of the Grenfell boys went a long way.[69] Nor were their friends universally admired. Duff Cooper recorded a description of them as "a speechless, noisy, drunken, audacious crew".[70]

Many others were members. They included Edward and Katharine Horner, Asquith's daughter. Edward was badly wounded in France but survived. Billy and Charles Lister, who joined the Labour Party and became a diplomat at the Rome Embassy; the three Manners girls; Edward Tennant, Margot's brother, later Lord Glenconner; Patrick Shaw Stewart, who worked for Baring's Bank; and later, Montagu. Almost all were to die in the war.

They rebelled against the constraints of their parents. In the last peaceful years before the war, they not only drank too much champagne but turned as well to morphia (morphine) and chlorers (chloroform) after dances or death of friends. They didn't merely flirt; they kissed and sometimes more than that. They evaded chaperones, shocked their parents, scandalised society, and sought to outdo their parents in flamboyance.[71] They held riotous parties. They were socially much in demand at dinners in London and at country house parties and enjoyed much the same pleasures as the Bright Young Things of the 1920s[72] Diana wrote: "The Coterie's pride was to be unafraid of words, unshocked by drink and unashamed of decadence and gambling … Unlike-Other-People, I'm afraid. Our peak of unpopularity was certainly 1914 and 1915."[73]

---

69 Ziegler, 47.

70 John Julius Norwich, ed., *The Duff Cooper Diaries 1915-1951* (London: Phoenix, 2006), 44.

71 Lambert, 149.

72 Artemis Cooper, *A Durable Fire* (London: Collins, 1983), xv.

73 Lady Diana Cooper, *The Rainbow Comes and Goes* (London: Rupert Hart Davis, 1958), 82.

The Prime Minister and His Mistress

On one occasion, Diana was dining with the Montagus and a message was sent to Savory and Moore in St James's requesting a supply of chloroform. They told the chemist that Diana was having trouble with her eye. The chemists informed Diana's mother. She arrived to find Diana's eyes in good health. Various improbable suggestions were made as to the necessity for the chloroform, ranging from her dog being in great pain, to Venetia having neuralgia, and finally, to Montagu being troubled by hay fever.[74] It was not only drugs which the Coterie were into. They drank a very great deal of champagne, sometimes vodka, sometimes absinthe, sometimes by itself, and sometimes with drugs.

Cynthia wrote, "I gained some lights on the creed of the Coterie. I am sure there is an insidiously corruptive poison in their minds … brilliantly distilled by their inspiration, Raymond. I don't care a damn about their morals and manners, but I do think what – for want of a better word – I call their anti-cant, is really suicidal to happiness."[75] Some idea of their behaviour can be gathered from the account which Cynthia received from a friend who had witnessed a wonderful Coterie episode. "After dinner", recorded Cynthia, "Diana ejaculated, 'I *must* be unconscious tonight', and away went a taxi to fetch chloroform from the chemist, 'Jolly old chlorers'! One guest who had nearly fainted at dinner had to be removed before the orgy began."[76] They pursued their activities not only during the war, but after the war. They were later described by Asquith in a letter to Hilda Harrisson as "a rotten social gang … who lead a futile and devastating life."

Asquith wrote three descriptions of Venetia. He called them "Portraits of a Lady" and he sent them to her. The first, dated 3 February 1915, reads:

---

74   Ziegler, 71.

75   Cynthia Asquith, 7.

76   Ibid. 112.

Sir Oliver Popplewell

"Portrait of a Lady

Mainly by herself

Tho' she had not by any means an exalted opinion of herself –indeed was singularly free of vanity except in one or two small things – she had no ambition to become better than or different from, what she was. Both by conviction and temperament, she was sceptical of what is called self improvement. And, unlike some people who are content with themselves, but consumed with missionary zeal, she never made any effort to correct the shortcomings, whether of character or of manners, of her associates or friends. She preferred, not out of laziness or lethargy, still less from want of perception, to take them as they stood, and to leave them as she found them. By nature, she was not passionate, and for that reason she was free from some of the temptations to which more susceptible and impressionable characters are exposed. When she was, for a moment, in doubt whether to do or abstain from doing anything, her decision was not as a rule determined by considerations of right or wrong; rather she was guided by what seemed to her at the time, being the easier and more convenient, even the more amusing or adventurous course. She was not the least selfish or egotistic: on the contrary she was without effort or self-suppression, kindly, considerate and generous and abounding in joie de vivre.... She was by no means simple, but (for a woman) exceptionally balanced and as a critic once said, "unsurprised," never more conspicuously so than in one episode in her life when she won, without seeking it for a moment, the passionate love and the unbroken confidence of a man much older than herself."

On 17 February, he wrote another portrait.

> "From the point of view of technical "religion," she offered little encouragement to the preachers and evangelists. She had "no sense of sin"; no penitential moods; no waves of remorse: no mystic reveries; no excursions (after the fashion of St Paul) into the Third Heaven, and hearing of "unspeakable words that it was not lawful for a man (or a woman) to utter" – The wings of her imagination – and it had wings as well as feet – when it left the ground took quite a different flight. Poetry and music fed & sustained it.
>
> She was not, as might seem from some phrases in what goes before, at all self complacent. She was genuinely sorry, if to please herself, she had disobliged or put off a friend. In argument, she was always ready (if convinced) to confess herself in the wrong. She hated quarrels and would sacrifice a strong position for the sake of "making it up" She had no rancours against people who had offended or wounded or slandered her; she was if anything forgiving to a fault. If asked whether she had any guiding principle, she would in some moods declare that it was to get "the maximum fun" out of life. In other moods, perhaps more often, she was inclined to doubt whether (in the words of a friend) "the quarry was worth the quest." She was preserved from cynicism and from living at hap-hazard by the native energy of a healthy temperament, and by a capacity for *real* devotion where she really cared."

His final description of her was contained in a letter which he wrote on 18 March.

"It was characteristic of her tendency to minimise moral dimensions, where she herself was concerned, that even when she took up unpalatable tasks (like hospital nursing) she quite sincerely disclaimed the imputation of "high-mindedness." She attributed her action not to unselfishness, or a sense of duty, or a desire to relieve suffering, but to the joint operation of two purely self-regarding motives; the one positive and the other negative. The positive motive, (so she declared,) was her calculation that she would emerge after three months of drudgery, with whetted appetite and zest for the pleasures of the world. The negative motive was that, during the three months, she would at any rate escape the more tiresome routine of daily life under war conditions in a country house.

When asked whether the interests of other people did not come in at all, she would reply that she had calculated that, on the whole, she would give as much pleasure to those she was fond of, and perhaps receive as much from them, in the one form of seclusion as in the other.... Nor was this attitude towards herself due in any way to a cynical temper. She had a rich capacity for admiration, was intensely ambitious for her friends, and, beyond measure, rejoiced at any recognition by the world of the qualities and faculties in them which had attracted herself."

At the same time, although not attracted to him, she had become seriously involved with Edwin Montagu.

CHAPTER FOUR

Montagu

 *E*dwin Montagu, who eventually married Venetia in 1915, had known her since before 1909, and thereafter their friendship flourished. By August 1912, he had summoned up enough courage to propose marriage to her, but she turned him down. He was then parliamentary under-secretary for India and was about to leave on a visit there. He seems not to have taken the rejection too hard, but determined thereafter to pursue the relationship. Venetia's attitude vacillated between rejection and acceptance on a compromise basis, meaning that it could be a friendship without sexual relations, because she found him physically unattractive. Their correspondence had continued until September 1912, during which time she indicated she might marry him, but in such Delphic terms that by the end of the month, he recognised that marriage was not a possibility. On 4 October 1912, he set sail for India. Montagu was then aged 32. His father, a very wealthy banker, had been created Lord Swaythling in 1907. He died in 1911, leaving his money in trust for his children. As a result, Montagu was now well off.

 Montagu had been variously educated. He started at Clifton College in 1891, but a combination of unhappiness and severe headaches caused his parents to remove him. In April 1893, he was sent to the City of London School, and from there, in 1895, he went to the University College in London. He secured a place at Trinity College, Cambridge, where he became chairman of the University Liberal Club and a distinguished president of the Union. After leaving Cambridge in

December 1905, he was adopted as Liberal candidate for Chesterton in West Cambridgeshire, and in 1906 became their MP. When Asquith became chancellor of the exchequer, Montagu was his private secretary, which post he retained when Asquith became prime minister. He was then successively parliamentary under-secretary of state for India from 1914, financial secretary to the treasury from 1914–15, and chancellor of the duchy of Lancaster from January 1915 with a place in the Cabinet. From 1914, he had resumed his friendship and correspondence with Venetia at the same time as she was having an affair with Asquith. In May 1915, when the coalition of Liberals and Conservatives was formed, he lost his seat in the Cabinet, and reverted to being financial secretary.

He played an important part in resolving one of the first problems facing the coalition government. This was the shortage of manpower, which resulted in a demand for conscription. The first step was taken in June 1915, when a registration bill was proposed. Conscription was an issue which fiercely divided the parties, both from each other and among themselves. Haldane, now removed from office, had been a strong protagonist, while Asquith was for a gradual approach. The Liberals and the Labour Party were ideologically opposed, as were the Irish Nationalists. Kitchener favoured a volunteer army. But events took over.

The failure of the landings in Gallipoli, and the disaster of the latest Allied offensive in France, with the British loss of 60,000 and the French of 150,000 men, necessitated a change of outlook. By the end of 1915, it was clear that the Derby scheme had failed. That was a rather complicated scheme under which men, both married and unmarried, were encouraged to attest by a government pledge that, unless all but a small number of single men came forward, compulsion would be imposed on them. Married men were to be separately treated. In the result, 650,000 remained unattested. When Asquith proposed the Military Services Bill, several of the Liberal ministers threatened to resign. In the result, however, only Sir John Simon did. It was partly due to Asquith's political deftness that the bill was passed, but others played their part.

Montagu, as Asquith told Sylvia on 2 January 1916, had been "indefatigable in helping to solve the conscription crisis. When the crisis was over, Margot ordered three green cigarette cases to be given to Reading, Hankey, and Montagu to thank them for their part in its resolution. She inscribed each to "a real friend from Margot Asquith, in memory of the last week in 1915".[77] But there were still problems. A further proposal was made that unattested married men were to be given a further opportunity to come forward, and unless 5,000 came forward before the end of May and some 15,000 a week thereafter, conscription would be imposed. On 25 May 1916, conscription was formally enacted.

The year 1916 saw an improvement in Montagu's career, because in January he re-entered the Cabinet and in June became Minister of Munitions, succeeding Lloyd George. When Kitchener died at sea on his way to Russia, HMS Hampshire having hit a mine in the North Sea, Lloyd George took over the War Office. By December, he had succeeded Asquith as Prime Minister. Montagu did his best to seek some sort of rapprochement between the two, but without success.

Montagu now ceased to be a minister. There are conflicting views about whether he was offered another post. It is believed that Bonar Law, on behalf of Lloyd George, offered Montagu the post of financial secretary to the treasury again, which he declined. Venetia told Duff Cooper that Lloyd George had offered Montagu the post of chancellor of the exchequer, but he had refused.[78]

Montagu himself makes some reference to the offer of a post in a memorandum dated 9 December 1916 in which he sought to justify what appeared to be his disloyalty to Asquith. He wrote, "I desire to place on record that I have not received any offer to join George's Government, but I know that that is because George did not want a refusal, and if, at any time, I had sent him a message to say that I would come in, I should have been invited to join."[79]

---

77   *Margot Asquith's Diary*, 119.

78   Norwich, 42.

79   Montagu Papers. Cambridge University Library, AS 1/10/1).

Montagu's disloyalty to Asquith in joining Lloyd George's side, which the Asquith family regarded as nothing less than treachery, was a constant source of complaint by all their members. The passage of time did nothing to assuage their anger. Cynthia wrote on 7 December: "went to see Venetia … she said Montagu had had dozens of frenzied letters from Margot full of insults 'I hear you are going in with them – where is friendship? Where is loyalty?' However, poor dear, he is not going in with them, though I believe suffering tortures in refusing. Apparently he is *sous le charme* of Lloyd George and could quite well go in with him as regards his own intellectual conscience, so it is a real sacrifice to personal loyalty."[80]

In 1917, the Asquiths were still upset about what they perceived as Montagu's betrayal. Cynthia again wrote, "We talked of the Asquiths' indignation at Montagu's so-called 'ratting' Margot was vehement about it, saying Venetia ought to leave him …"[81] Violet too could not believe that someone who owed so much to Asquith could possibly have behaved as badly as Montagu had.

Nor did her attitude towards Montagu soften with time. In 1920, with the Liberals now divided into two factions, there were disputes over the control of constituency parties. At Oxford, Montagu had sought to secure the constituency for Lloyd George's faction as against the Asquithian liberals. On 24 January 1920, Violet wrote a letter to Sir Gilbert Murray, the distinguished professor of Greek, at Oxford University, and the chairman of the League of Nations Union. He had been the unsuccessful Liberal candidate for Oxford University in the parliamentary elections. The letter read:

> "Dear Professor Murray, Thank you so much for your letter – & its news. Et tu Judas! I didn't know that it was in me to form an even lower estimate of Montagu's character than I held already – but it has happened. That he should

---

[80] Cynthia Asquith, 244.

[81] Cynthia Asquith, 326.

> offer himself as the catspaw for LlG. to undercut the position of the Free Liberals generally – & Father in particular – in what is thanks to you – one of our few strongholds – is really <u>incredible</u> – especially as whenever he meets a member of our entourage … he pours out to them a plaint about his present leader & political environment … insists that Father is his "spiritual home" & that he is on the verge of resigning and returning to the fold. His <u>cant</u> & cringing dishonesty make me quite sick."[82]

Even in 1949, Margot could not leave the sore alone. She sent a letter to a Mr Roberts with a copy of Montagu's memorandum of 9 December, adding: "He [Montagu] had remarkable qualities, but loyalty to a great leader or any consideration for his party, if either stood in the way of his career, were not among his virtues."[83] Violet also wrote:

> "After my Father's fall from power, Jack Seely lent us for a few weeks his house on the Isle of Wight and I wrote to Edwin [Montagu] asking him which weekends he would like to spend with us there. To my amazement, he replied that he was engaged for all of them and could not come at all. This was to me the first shock of realisation, and, from that moment, I understood his one desire was to get back into the Government, any Government, at any price and on any terms. This, as you know, he did.[84]

Margot, too, had earlier expressed the view that by urging Asquith to compromise with Lloyd George, Montagu had given him the most rotten advice. Even six years after his defection, she still felt incensed at the behaviour of those whom she thought had deserted her husband. She wrote, "Today [1922] I can write with calm of these events, but at the

---

[82] *Champion Redoubtable*, 108.
[83] Asquith Papers. Bodleian Library, Oxford. AS.7.170.
[84] Ibid.

time of their occurrence, I was shocked and wounded by the meanness, ingratitude, and lack of loyalty shown to a man who in all the years he had been Prime Minister had disproved these qualities in a high degree.... My husband fell on the battlefield surrounded by civilians and soldiers, whom he had fought for and saved; some of whom owed him not only their reputations and careers but their very existence. Only a handful of faithful men remained by his side to see whether he was killed or wounded, and on 7th of December Mr Lloyd George became Prime Minister."[85]

In June 1917, Montagu was offered the post of the secretary of state for India and accepted. It was to prove a poisoned chalice. His public life, like his private life, fell into a slow decline. The post became available when Austin Chamberlain, the previous holder of the office, resigned after the publication of the Mesopotamian Report. This report had investigated the circumstances surrounding the humiliating defeat of British and Indian troops by the Turks in September 1915 at Kut. Six thousand Indian and two thousand British troops surrendered, and many died in captivity. The report blamed the defeat on the military incompetence in India and particularly on the viceroy and commander-in-chief in India. Montagu attacked Chamberlain, not only about the report itself, but about the whole attitude of the India Office to the problems of India. Chamberlain rather unexpectedly resigned. Montagu had been eager to re-enter the government for some time. He had thought in June that in view of his work on the reconstruction committee, he would become minister for reconstruction.

When he wrote to Asquith explaining his reasons for seeking the post, he got a pretty dusty reply. Asquith wrote back, "Thank you for your letter of yesterday. In view of our past relations, it is not unnatural that I should find it difficult to understand, and still more difficult to appreciate, your reasons for the course which you tell me you propose to take. But in these matters every man must be guided by his own judgement and conscience."[86]

---

85   Margot Asquith, *Autobiography*, ii. 246–247.

86   Montagu, AS 6/11/7.

Others had the same view. Frances Stevenson, Lloyd George's mistress and subsequently his wife, recorded: "D [Lloyd George] says he does not like his [Montagu's] readiness to turn his back on Asquith. He says if it had not been for Asquith, Montagu would never have been heard of – that he is purely a man who was made by Asquith. But Montagu has no scruples in deserting his benefactor and going over to the other side as soon as it suits his interests to do so."

Frances Stevenson further recorded in her diary:

> "I loathe Montagu – I should call him the most insignificant but most ambitious of Cabinet Ministers, differing from the majority of the others in that he has in, an enormous degree, the "push" ... I do not trust the man, I feel that he is insincere & a hanger on.... Montagu still writes letters every day to D in a crawling style, ending up nearly every time with "God Bless you," and this when we certainly know that he is intriguing the whole time behind D's back ... Personally I hate the idea of Montagu hanging around. He is not to be trusted & I feel sure he is a spy. I spoke to D about it but he said "Don't you worry: I know my Montagu; I only tell him things that I want Asquith to know!"[87]

If the Asquiths had seen a letter which Montagu had written to Lloyd George a few weeks earlier, all possibility of reconciliation would have gone. It read:

> "I am anxious to be the forerunner of young Liberals who will flock to your standard. After all, my friendship with Asquith is well known. I am prepared to leave him because I find that I am in agreement with you in your aims and in disagreement with those who I now find to

---

[87] Frances Stevenson, *Lloyd George: A Diary* (London: Hutchinson & Co., 1971), 40, 51, 114, 139.

be my colleagues in the House of Commons. When I come to you, you will be my only political friend in the Coalition Government. Let us have an opportunity of working and sticking together."[88]

But unfortunately for him, chance was to ensure that on a number of occasions he was to choose a course contrary to the policy of the government of which he was a member, and which cumulatively eventually led to his downfall.

The first occasion was his opposition to the Balfour Declaration published on 31 October 1917. It was designed to express the government's view about the prospect of providing the Jewish nation with a homeland. It was addressed to Lord Rothschild, with a request that he should it bring it to the attention of the Zionist Federation.

> "His Majesty's Government views with favour the establishment of a national home for the Jewish people and will use their best endeavours to facilitate the achievement of this object, it being clearly understood that nothing shall be done which may prejudice the civil and religious rights of non-Jewish communities in Palestine, or the rights and political status enjoyed by Jews in any other country."

Montagu's objection was that the declaration would provide a rallying ground for anti-Semites in every country in the world.[89]

The next problem confronting Montagu was how to deal with the demand in India for self-governing institutions with a view to the progressive realisation of responsible government as an integral part of the British Empire. This was a fine ideal but almost impossible to translate into practice, given the intractable views of those closely involved, both in Britain and in India. Thus, it was not until the 1930s that any serious

---

88   Levine, 407.

89   Ibid. 435.

progress was made, and only in 1946 was full independence granted. Montagu and the viceroy, Lord Chelmsford, produced a report in April 1918 that recommended various modest reforms. Curzon, who had been viceroy himself from 1899–1905, was critical, and while the Cabinet agreed to publish the report, they were not very enthusiastic about progressing it. By this time, the war was coming to an end. The terms of the peace treaties and a general election were now to dominate the political scene.

Before the election, Lloyd George decided that those liberals who had supported him in the "Maurice debate" should have the support of the coalition, while those who had voted against the government should not. It became known as the Coupon Election. The Maurice debate arose from an article published in May 1918 by General Sir Frederick Maurice, suggesting that the government had kept the army short of troops. After a stormy debate, Lloyd George won the vote, with the help of some highly doubtful statistics. Montagu had no difficulty in remaining in Lloyd George's camp and was returned at the general election with an increased majority. The coalition won 474 seats (the Conservatives 338 and the Liberals 136). The Asquithian Liberals won only 26 seats. Asquith lost the seat which he had held for thirty-two years.

After the election, Montagu was reappointed as secretary of state for India and was invited to be India's representative at the Peace Conference. Unfortunately, he and Lloyd George differed as to Montagu's responsibilities there. Montagu saw his function as representing India's views, separate from the views of the British delegation, if they happened to differ. Montagu was particularly concerned that the peace terms imposed on Muslim Turkey should not be too harsh because of the risk that the Muslims in India might be upset.[90] He wrote an endless stream of memoranda on the subject to Lloyd George and others.[91] But Lloyd George was determined to go his own way on the subject of Turkey, and Montagu found himself being sidelined in discussions.

---

90 Montagu, AS 4/4/12.

91 Ibid., AS 4/4/9. AS 3/3/1(7). AS 4/6/5. AS 4/3/7. AS 4/3/8. AS 4/6/11.

By March 1919, he was having difficulty in being able to express the Indian view to the British delegation at the Peace conference. When he complained that Lloyd George had given him a pledge that the views of the Indian delegation would be sent to President Wilson, Hankey (the Cabinet secretary) told him that if India were to be consulted, every little power would also want to be consulted. In addition to his views on Turkey and on other countries in the Middle East, Montagu was concerned as was Keynes about the reparations being demanded from Germany. On 4 April, he wrote a private memorandum to Lloyd George full of pent-up fury at having his opinions totally ignored. "I have not at any stage or any time been allowed to express an opinion, been informed officially, been consulted upon affairs in Mesopotamia, Syria, Arabia or Palestine. I do not know what is occurring. I cannot accept responsibility.... As regards the Peace – I had no share in, nor was I consulted on policy", referring to the question of reparations in the peace treaty with Germany.[92] He told Lloyd George that he could not accept the proposed terms of the peace treaty with Turkey because of the effect on the Mohammedan population of India.[93] In December, Montagu wrote yet again to Lloyd George on the same subject and circulated a memorandum to the Cabinet, pointing out that a number of distinguished and influential people in India, like the viceroy, the Indian government, the native princes, and both Muslims and Hindus, took the same view as he did.[94]

In April 1920, there was to be a conference at San Remo on the Turkish peace treaty. Montagu wanted his views distributed to the conference if he would not be allowed to be present, but Curzon was sent as the only British representative to accompany Lloyd George. His idea of a memorandum to the conference was rejected. When Montagu protested that India's views would not be properly represented and that Lloyd George was reneging on an undertaking that India would have separate representation, he was

---

92   Ibid., AS 1/12/18.

93   India Foreign Office, F/40/2/48.

94   Montagu, AS 4/8/96.

sharply rebuked.[95] Lloyd George's dislike for Turkey and his enthusiasm for the Greeks was eventually to result in the breakup of the coalition government and to his permanent loss of office.

Events in India were also to have an adverse effect on Montagu's future. In April 1919, there had been riots in many parts of India, but it was at Amritsar on 13 April that an event occurred which was to cast a deep shadow over Anglo–Indian relations for generations. On 10 April, a crowd at Amritsar tried to force their way across a bridge. Shots were fired by soldiers. The crowd melted away, but they soon returned in greater numbers and again tried to cross the bridge. This time they were successful. They wrecked the telephone exchange. There was looting and arson, and a number of people were killed. On 12 April, troops under General Dyer announced an 8 p.m. curfew. On 13 April, some 20,000 demonstrators gathered peacefully in a yard. Dyer ordered his troops to open fire on the unarmed crowd. They killed over 350 demonstrators and wounded nearly four times that number. In addition, orders were given by Dyer that if any Indians wanted to use the particular street where an English lady missionary had been knocked down during earlier rioting, they would have to crawl on their hands and knees. Eventually, a committee of inquiry was set up under the chairmanship of Lord Hunter.

While that was taking place, Montagu had the satisfaction of piloting his India Reform Bill through Parliament. This was to pave the way eventually (albeit at a snail's pace) for some form of self-government. It had been an ambition of Montagu's for some time to be viceroy of India. Given his previous offices and experience, he believed himself to be uniquely qualified for the position. In January 1920, he wrote a long letter to Lloyd George setting out his vision for India and emphasising his particular qualifications.[96] Lloyd George was non-committal, and it gradually dawned on Montagu that he was never going to be offered the post. Later in 1920, he started to suggest other names and eventually withdrew his own.

---

95 Ibid., AS 1/12/67

96 Ibid., AS 4/3/32.

In May 1920, Hunter's report was published. It gave rise to heated parliamentary debates, in which a now hostile Conservative attack on Montagu's integrity took place. A motion to reduce his salary (a parliamentary device for passing a vote of no confidence in a minister) was proposed. Rupert Gwynne, MP for Eastbourne, spoke for many of Montagu's detractors when he said, "the right hon. Gentleman's administration of affairs in India is a much greater danger to that country.... I have tried to elicit certain information from the right hon. Gentleman in this House and I regret to say he has misinformed this House. He has said, and repeated, on more than one occasion, things which I can prove are not true, and if that is so, anyone occupying the great position which the right hon. Gentleman does, is not fit to be Secretary of State for India … If the right hon. Gentleman continues, we are going on the right road to losing India. The most graceful thing he could do now, would be to resign."[97]

The Liberals did little to support Montagu. Although the vote of no confidence was lost by nearly 2–1, Lloyd George now recognised that Montagu was a liability to the government, more particularly as some of the Conservatives were beginning to question the wisdom of remaining in the coalition. The situation in India did not improve when Lord Reading became the viceroy.

In February 1920, Montagu again found himself the subject of a motion of no confidence for his actions during the previous three years. Montagu's liberal views about the future of India and his failure to curb the civil disobedience campaign of Gandhi were among the chief criticisms by Conservative diehards. But the language used by his critics reflected the fact that it was Montagu's own personality which was under attack, as well as his policies.

"There was a debate in the Legislative Assembly [in India] yesterday," said Sir William Joynson-Hicks, MP for Twickenham:

> "where all the non-official members led by some of the extremists in that Assembly … one and all passed

---

97 *H o C Debates*, 5th Series, cxxxi. pars. 1795, 1803.

encomiums on the right hon. Gentleman, that he was the most wonderful man who had ever ruled India, and that they would regard it as an affront to India if we were to pass this Amendment. He was the most popular man in India. I do not deny that he is the most popular man with the extremists. If Gandhi is a friend of his, he is a friend of Gandhi.... I do not deny that all the extremists from one end of India to the other would desire him to remain as Secretary of State and to remain at the head of the supine policy which has led India to the position it is in today."[98]

Lloyd George did little to defend Montagu. Of Joynson-Hicks' speech, he said, "I am very delighted, as an old friend to congratulate my hon. Friend upon his speech.... He spoke with moderation and restraint. He avoided, at any rate, any petty personalities, and his speech was all the stronger for that reason."[99] Lloyd George heard only part of Joynson-Hicks' speech, which may help to explain his astonishing view that Joynson-Hicks had avoided "personalities", petty or otherwise.

Gwynne followed Joynson–Hicks. His speech, too, Lloyd George found moderate. Gwynne continued his attack from the previous debate. "The appalling muddle which has been taking place in India during his tenure of office would have caused any ordinary individual to resign 20 or 30 times, but he sits there unmoved, putting the blame on anyone he can ... doing anything to save his own skin."[100]

Gwynne went on: "At all times, the right hon. Gentleman remains in the background. He is working underground. His methods remind one of those of a mole." After referring to a gardener's view that a mole has a thin skin, he continued:

---

98 Ibid., pars. 872–873.

99 Ibid., pars. 954–955.

100 Ibid., par. 884.

"That is not one of the characteristics possessed by the right hon. Gentleman. His skin is not too thin. Indeed I doubt if a hippopotamus has a thicker skin than the right hon. Gentleman, … After the last Debate … I asked other members whether they did not share my views. In two days no fewer than 93 Members signed this petition to the Prime Minister "We the undersigned, being of the opinion that the Secretary of State for India has lost the confidence of a large number of members of the House of Commons and of the country, and that the continuance in office would be detrimental to the best interests of this country and of India, think it desirable that he should vacate his present office.""

Gwynne finished by saying, "They [Members of the House] regard it as an insult that anyone who has brought such blunders, such disgrace upon the Government of this country, should still remain in office."[101]

In the same debate, Lord Percy came to Montagu's rescue and expressed the view of those undecided. "There are many in this House who do not belong to the company of the Mover and Seconder, who are in grave doubt … as to how to vote if this Amendment were carried to a Division. That doubt, however, has been entirely eliminated by the tone of the speeches made in support of it. It is quite impossible for us to vote in favour of an Amendment couched in those terms, more especially after it has been recommended to us by the kind of speech which has been delivered by the Hon Member for Eastbourne [Mr Gwynne]."[102]

Another member had the courage to speak of the reasons behind the bitter attacks on Montagu. The Right Honourable Francis Acland said, "I believe that these personal attacks on the Secretary of State are

---

101 Ibid., pars. 889–891.

102 Ibid., par. 942.

based very largely not on sober and careful consideration of the position in India, but on religious prejudices, which ought to be unknown when serious matters of this kind are in issue."[103] Still another member pointed out that "My right Hon Friend, [Montagu] very successfully and very properly protested against the introduction of the personal element...."[104] Again Montagu won the vote on the censure motion. However, his euphoria was not to last very long.

On 28 February, Reading sent Montagu a telegram urging that the Treaty of Sevres (the peace treaty with Turkey) be revised and seeking permission to publish the telegram with his reasons in full "forthwith."[105] Montagu circulated the telegram to his Cabinet colleagues on a Saturday afternoon. Reading sent a further telegram saying that in view of the imminent arrest of Gandhi, it was essential that the telegram should be published immediately, because it would help satisfy Mohammedan anxiety about the Turkish treaty. In fact it contained little new. Montagu gave Reading that permission. When the Cabinet met on Monday, ministers were surprised to find that without their knowledge or approval the telegram had already been published.[106] When Lloyd George, who had not been at the Cabinet meeting on the Monday, read the story in a newspaper, he interviewed Montagu. He subsequently sent him a letter on 9 March, 1922 in which he wrote "... that you were actuated in the course which you pursued solely by a sense of public duty, I do not for a moment doubt. Nevertheless, the fact remains that without being urged by any pressing necessity and without consulting either the Cabinet or Foreign Secretary or myself or anyone of my colleagues, you caused to be published a telegram from the Viceroy raising questions whose importance extends far beyond the frontiers of India or your office.... the public consequences of this course of action must inevitably be serious; its effect upon your colleagues,

---

103 Ibid., pars. 995–996.

104 Ibid., pars. 925–926.

105 Montagu, AS 1/12/100.

106 Levine, 629–631.

is I need hardly say, painful in the extreme. In these circumstances, I cannot doubt that you will share my view that after what has occurred, we cannot usefully cooperate in the same Cabinet."[107]

Lloyd George's attitude towards Montagu can be deduced from a letter he sent to Frances Stevenson in March. "Montagu is a swine of a sneak. When I come back I'll re-circumcise him."[108] On 9 March, Montagu resigned office.

Meanwhile Lloyd George's desire to champion Greece against Turkey almost involved Britain in another war. For this and for other reasons, the Conservatives decided that they had had enough of the Coalition. On 19 October 1922, at a meeting at the Carlton Club, they voted to leave the Coalition and fight the forthcoming election as an independent party. Lloyd George resigned. Bonar Law became prime minister. At the general election in November, the Conservatives won 344 seats, Labour 138, Lloyd George's Liberals 57, and Asquith Liberals 60. The Liberals were to be out of power for nearly 90 years.

Asquith, who had won Paisley in 1920 at a by-election, held on to his seat but with a reduced majority. He was re-elected in 1924. Montagu was defeated in 1922 and did not stand again. On 15 November 1924, aged 45, he died.

After he died, Venetia wrote to Asquith:

> "My dearest Mr Asquith, We found this letter for you among Edwin's papers, written I think just before he went to India. I know it is not necessary to tell you how deeply he loved you and what a lasting grief your political separation was. He always used to say that tho' he was absorbingly interested in his work after he left you, it was no longer any fun.... Thank you for all you did to make his life happy. He was always grateful to you. All my love. *Venetia*"

---

107 MG (The Letters, manuscripts and other materials in the possession of Milton Gendel, husband of the late Judith Gendel at his home in Rome. 9 March 1922.)

108 A.J.P. Taylor, ed., *My Darling Pussy* (London: Weidenfeld and Nicolson, Ltd., 1975), 36.

A few days later she wrote again:

> "My darling Mr Asquith, Edwin asked me to give you something of his and I finally thought you might like this Hamlet which I had given him a long time ago. I never thanked you for your divine letter, you know how dumb and inarticulate I am, but you do realise, I hope, how glad I was to get it. I hope I may see you sometime, when you get back. Much love always, *Venetia*."[109]

Montagu's marriage to Venetia had been full of difficulties from the outset, and they continued throughout their married life. It is an important part of the story, because her subsequent behaviour with other men throws some light on her previous affair with Asquith.

Venetia found Montagu physically unattractive. In May 1915, Violet recorded:

> "Curious and disturbing news reached us on Wed. evening of Montagu's engagement to Venetia.… I am bound to confess that the thought of it … much as I love him – and clearly as I recognise his points – filled me with horror. The reasons against are too obvious to require definition & I had reason to believe from things she [Venetia] has said to me in the past that she was fully alive to them. M's physical repulsiveness to me is such that I wd lightly leap from the top story of Queen Anne's Mansions or the Eiffel Tower itself, to avoid the slightest contact – the thought of any erotic amenities with him is enough to freeze one's blood."[110]

---

[109] Jenkins, 510.

[110] *Champion Redoubtable*, 49–50.

This was a common view of Montagu.[111] Others did not think that Venetia "was in love in any sense of the word".[112]

An equally important obstacle to their getting married was the proviso which Swaythling had attached to his will. This stipulated that if any of his children abandoned the Jewish faith or married out of it, they would lose their inheritance. Thus on the one hand, unless Venetia embraced the Jewish faith, marriage to Montagu would result in their living in comparative poverty. On the other hand, there was also no doubt pressure on Venetia by her contemporaries not to flout convention by converting to Judaism. Montagu referred to this problem in a letter which he wrote to Venetia in April 1915. "But all I ask, when we are attacked or scorned, you regard yourself as one of us by adoption … Let them say what they like."

Ever since 1912, when she had turned down his proposal of marriage, Montagu still hoped that she would change her mind. He therefore continued to conduct a correspondence with Venetia parallel to Asquith's, but without success until 1915, when on 12 May, she wrote to Asquith to tell him of her engagement to Montagu. Asquith replied on the same day, "Most Loved – as you know well, *this* breaks my heart. I couldn't bear to come and see you. I only pray God to bless you – and help me. – Yours"

On 14 May Asquith wrote again. "This is too terrible! No Hell can be as bad. Cannot you send me one word? It is so unnatural. Only one word?" When Venetia replied with a "most revealing and heart rending letter", Asquith wrote on 17 May, "What am I to say? What can I say? I was able to keep silence for the two most miserable days of my life and then it became unbearable; and like you I felt it was cruel and unnatural and that anything was better. So I scrawled my 2 or 3 agonised sentences, and thank God you once more speak to me and I to you." He then suggested that she should take time before making any irrevocable decision.

---

111 Ibid. 63.

112 Ibid. 59.

There was further correspondence between Asquith and Venetia about her engagement to Montagu. She criticized Asquith for judging her by harsh standards but nevertheless continued to express her desire to see him. He said it soothed his "sore heart" and he wrote: "I think I *must* see you on Monday before you go [to France]."

In another letter he wrote, "I *must see you* before you go. I know it will be painful but I must tell you why. I think you and I ought to face it." He went on:

> "So, at whatever cost to both of us, I feel that in loyalty to our past, I must come and tell you the real & whole truth. I go to the Wharf for Sunday – late Sat – but I shall be back fairly early on Monday. Have you then a half hour? I don't know yet whether we (you & I), have a real future. That will come clearer to me in time. But I am quite resolved that our *past* shall not be spoiled but "orb into the perfect star" … Is there anyone – even yourself – who knows *how much* I love you? It will *never* be told …"

On 22 May, he wrote again suggesting a meeting, and they met for a farewell half hour on 23 May. On 24 May, she left to go to Wimereux, near Boulogne, where she was due to spend a month as a nurse in Lady Norman's hospital.

On 29 May, Montagu went to see Asquith to discuss his engagement to Venetia. Montagu described the visit in a letter to her on 31 May. "He [Asquith] was just too noble and splendid for words.… he had only doubts if change of religion was too much like a transaction and he feared we would not be happy … all he minded were his doubts as to our love. He told me he hoped and prayed his doubts were not well founded and ended by blessing me and wishing us both well."

Asquith arranged to see Venetia at Boulogne on his way back from a visit to the Western Front. But before they met he wrote to her, reaffirming his one prayer that she should be happy and ending "*tout passé, tout casse, tout lasse.*" (Everything passes, everything breaks, everything wears out.) She told him that she was determined to go ahead with the religious conversion and that the marriage would not weaken.

On 3 June, she wrote that she hoped that he would not allow the marriage to disrupt their friendship. Asquith's reply was dated 11 June.

> "Most loved ... I thought it better for both of us that I should think about it [her letter] and the whole agonising problems wh. it raises, before writing an answer. That fact, in itself, is almost too tragic for words. For the best part of three years, it has been so natural & easy and inevitable for me to write to you – every day, twice a day; if opportunity had offered, at every hour of the day or night.... You were the centre & mainspring of my life: everything in it hung on you; there was not an act or a thought (as you knew well) wh I did not share with you.... but your letter (quite a divine one, worthy in every way of my loved & worshipped Venetia) is addressed not to the unforgettable past but to the undisclosed & impenetrable future.... But how can you think it possible – you don't, I know – that things can ever again be as they were? I had the *best* that a man had or could have. Don't for God's sake think me selfish or exorbitant if I shrink from the second best.... Don't force me to sadder and adamantine resolutions.... Don't think me hard if I seem, for the time, to stand aloof. Don't press me now to say anything – except that I love you – always – everywhere. Your heart – broken and *ever devoted*. My very dearest – I hope this won't give you as much pain to read as it has given me to write it. I love you."

He continued writing to Venetia from time to time and he gave an impression to one observer of not being too unhappy.[113] On 7 July 1915, the *Jewish Chronicle* stated that "the Hon. Venetia Stanley who

---

113 *Champion Redoubtable*, 69.

is engaged to the Hon Edwin Montagu, has become a member of the Jewish community, having adopted the Jewish faith."[114] Asquith saw her in July when she called to see Violet, and he sent her two silver boxes as a wedding present, which were chosen by her sister, Sylvia, with whom Asquith was now in fairly frequent correspondence. His letter to Venetia accompanying the boxes read, "with all my love and more wishes than words can frame for your complete and unbroken happiness".[115]

He wrote to Venetia three times in July, including a farewell letter on 24 July 1915, just before her wedding. "I treasure as among the best things that any companionship could give, unforgettable and undying memories, and that I pray without ceasing to 'whatever god there be' that you may have a complete, and (so far as maybe) an unclouded life. Will you always remember an old & favourite text of mine (on which I never found it necessary to preach to you). 'It is the Spirit which prevaileth.' Always and everywhere *Your Loving*."

He wrote to her once in October and in November, and twice in December, mainly in answer to letters from her. They had already met on 13 September (the day after Asquith's birthday) in North Berwick. Venetia was persuaded to stay for dinner and leave by the night train. Cynthia Asquith recorded, "Venetia went away at ten to eleven. We were all delightedly amused by the idea of her travelling down with the P.M. ... funny enough! It will be almost their first meeting since the breach."[116]

Although Venetia and Asquith met subsequently at various social functions.[117] that was the end of their relationship. In November 1927, he had a final meeting with Venetia when he went to stay a night with her at Breccles Hall, the Montagu home in Norfolk. His final letter to her, dated 11 November, reads: "Dearest – it was with a sad heart and heavy

---

114 *Times*, 17 July 1915, 7.

115 Jenkins, 365.

116 Cynthia Asquith, 79.

117 Cynthia Asquith, 106–107, 119. Norwich, 24, 40. *The Rainbow*, 148. Clifford, 382. Mary Soames, *Clementine Churchill* (Boston: Houghton, Mifflin Co., 1979), 201.

feet that I turned my back on Breccles. I have enjoyed every minute of my little visit & long to come again when the flowers are all out. It was most good of you to take me in 'a sheer hulk' in need of refitting in your sheltered and delightful haven.... give my love to your Judith [Venetia's daughter] whose acquaintance I should like to improve. Much love. Yrs always. H"

In February 1928, he died. Venetia lived on for another twenty years until she too died, in August 1948. Her obituary in the *Times* is totally silent about her friendship with Asquith and suggests, contrary to the views of her contemporaries, that she supported Montagu when he resigned and that his death was a great blow to her.[118]

Overwhelmed with anguish in his private life, Asquith was now confronted with a serious crisis in his political life. On 17 May 1915, Asquith was forced to agree to reconstruct the government and to enter into a Coalition with the Unionists. The problems which resulted from the government's infirmity of purpose had been brewing for some months. There were two immediate catalysts for change. They were the problem of munitions and the turmoil at the Admiralty. The former was highlighted by what was generally perceived to be Asquith's misleading speech at Newcastle on 20 April in which he had suggested that there were no real problems about the provision of ammunition for the BEF. On 1 May, the leader in the *Daily Express* read: "such speeches as that delivered by Mr Asquith, a speech calculated to lull the nation into a fool's paradise ... are mischievous to a degree.... The country does not yet realise the significance of the War and the fault is the Government's."[119]

This was followed by a devastating attack in the *Times* on 14 May by the paper's military correspondent, Colonel Repington, and by a critical editorial. Repington's article carried the headlines: "NEED FOR SHELLS – BRITISH ATTACKS HELD – LIMITED SUPPLY THE CAUSE – A LESSON FROM FRANCE." He wrote:

---

118 *Times*, 7 August 1948, 6.

119 *Daily Express*, 18 May 1915.

> "The result of our attacks on Sunday last in the district of Fremeilles and Richebourg were disappointing. We found the enemy much more strongly posted than we expected. We had not sufficient high explosive to level his parapets to the ground after the French practice, and when our infantry gallantly stormed the trenches, as they did in both attacks, they found a garrison undismayed, many entanglements still intact and maxims on all sides ready to pour in streams of bullets.... The want of an unlimited supply of high explosive was a fatal bar to our success.

He compared this with the French practice on another sector at the front.

> By dint of the expenditure of 276 rounds of high explosive per gun in one day, all the German defences were levelled with the ground.... until we are thoroughly equipped for this trench warfare, we attack under grave disadvantages.... If we can break through the hard outer core of the German defences, we believe that we can scatter the German Armies ... but to break this hard core we need more high explosives, more heavy howitzers, more men.... it is certain that we can smash the German crust if we have the means. So the means we must have and as quickly as possible"[120]

The leading article was no less critical. It described heavy losses and an attack which led to nothing tangible because shells was lacking, and went on to say, "The reiterated appeals of our military correspondent make painful reading.... British troops died in vain on the Aubers Ridge on Sunday because more shells were needed. Our Government, who have so seriously failed to organise adequately our national resources, must bear their share of the grave responsibility."[121]

---

120 *Times*, 14 May 1915, 8.

121 Ibid. 9.

Like the munitions crisis, the turmoil at the Admiralty had been brewing for some months. It was due to the powerful and conflicting personalities of the two most senior office holders at the Admiralty, namely Churchill, First Lord of the Admiralty, and Lord Fisher, First Sea Lord. The problem was described by Asquith in two letters he wrote to Venetia on 20 January.

> "Hankey came to me today to say – *very privately* – that Fisher, who is an old friend of his, had come to him in a very unhappy frame of mind. He likes Winston personally, but complains, on purely technical naval matters, he is frequently over-ruled ("he out argues me"!) and he is not by any means at ease about either the present disposition of the fleets, or of their future movements.... Tho', I think the old man is rather unbalanced, I fear there is some truth in what he says; and I am revolving in my mind whether I can do anything, & if anything what? What do you say?"

On 28 January he wrote again on the subject to Venetia.

> "Another personal matter which rather troubles me is the growing friction between Winston and Fisher. They came to see me this morning before the War Council, and gave tongue to their mutual grievances. I tried to compose their differences by a compromise, under which Winston would give up for the present, his bombardment of Zeebrugge [Belgium], Fisher withdrawing his opposition to the operation against the Dardanelles. When at the Council we came to discuss the latter – wh. is warmly supported by Kitchener and Grey and enthusiastically by A.J.B.[alfour]… old "Jacky" [Fisher] maintained an obstinate and ominous silence. He is always threatening to resign, & and writes an

almost daily letter to Winston, expressing his desire to return to the cultivation of his "roses at Richmond" K[itchener] has taken on the role of conciliator, for wh. you might think, he was not naturally cut out!

Between January and May, relations between the two men worsened. The attempt to force the Dardanelles by ship had had to be abandoned, and any idea of further naval involvement was rejected. In April, the army had made its first landings at Gallipoli. There was stiff resistance, and casualties were heavy. In May, *Queen Elizabeth*, the flagship of the expedition was withdrawn, "as near a confession of failure as can easily be imagined." In these circumstances, the tension within the Admiralty increased to breaking point, and Churchill's reputation outside (and particularly with the Conservatives) plunged downwards.[122]

On 14 May, the mercurial Fisher made good his threat to resign and left the Admiralty. Violet gave a rather dramatic description of this episode.

> "Father ... told me an astonishing piece of news in these words "Fisher has levanted." He had simply <u>run away</u> from the Admiralty ... leaving his post, his work etc – pulling down all the blinds of his London House & leaving a red herring trail in the direction of Scotland.

His letter of resignation to Churchill had ended, "I am off to Scotland so as to avoid all questioning." He had in fact taken himself off to the Charing Cross Hotel. Violet continued

> "Masterton [Fisher's private secretary] expected him to be making for France & was out after him with a troop of beagles, scouring the continental railway stations and expresses. Lloyd George was off on another track and Bongie [Bonham Carter], on a 3rd.... Finally, however

---

122 Jenkins, 354-355.

he – Fisher was caught – carried in one of the retriever's mouths & dropped, bloodshot & panting, at the door of the Cabinet room.! Father had armed the beagles with a paper saying "Lord Fisher in the name of the King, I command you to return to your post." This writ was served on him! Father spent about an hour in conversation with him – he was very mellow and friendly but said he found W[inston] quite impossible to work with. He was always doing things without consulting him [F] … was overbearing etc"[123]

Although Fisher subsequently reappeared, his demand for the curtailment of Churchill's powers and for the dismissal of the rest of the Admiralty Board, convinced Asquith of the necessity to let Fisher go.

The combination of the munitions crisis and the turmoil at the Admiralty led the press and the Conservative opposition to demand a coalition government in which they expected to play a leading role. In the result, Asquith reconstructed his government. At the insistence of the Conservatives, Churchill was forced to leave the Admiralty. Due to a wicked press campaign about his philosophical attachment to Germany, Haldane, Asquith's long time friend, was removed from the office of lord chancellor. The break-up of the Coalition coincided with Venetia's engagement to Montagu and the end of Asquith's relationship with Venetia.

---

123 *Champion Redoubtable*, 50.

The Prime Minister and His Mistress

Asquith & Venetia

CHAPTER FIVE

The Nature of the Relationship

The relationship between Asquith and Venetia has given rise, unsurprisingly, to considerable speculation as to its nature. Some critics contend that this was a platonic friendship, similar to his friendship with other ladies to whom he had also written extensively. Others take a more cynical view. It is important to appreciate that however distinguished historians or the authors of articles or books are, their conclusions are only as good as the evidence on which their conclusions are based. Thus it is vital to take into account not only the direct evidence from witnesses, even though some of it is unsurprisingly contradictory, but perhaps more importantly, to weigh up the inferences to be drawn from the various strands of the relationship.

The Brocks, who first published Asquith's letters to Venetia in 1982, came to the conclusion that "it is almost certain that Asquith never became Venetia's lover in the physical sense, and it is unlikely that he even wished for this."[124] They added that "not being a love affair in the physical sense, it did not follow any recognisable sequence of passion or satiety."[125] No evidence to support this conclusion has been disclosed. Likewise, Roy Jenkins, a distinguished politician and the author of a number of well-received political biographies, described it as an epistolary relationship and "one which was a solace and relaxation

---

124 Brock, Michael and Eleanor.(Ed) *H.H. Asquith. Letters to Venetia Stanley.* (O.U.P. 1982) p 3.

125 Ibid. 13.

interfering with his duties no more than did Lloyd George's hymn singing or Churchill's late-night conversation."[126] He, too, provides no evidence for arriving at this strange conclusion. When he wrote the revised edition of *Asquith* in 1978, Violet, the stout defender of her father's reputation, was still alive. Although "she did not exactly exercise censorship",[127] she surely had some influence on his conclusions. Also, his own strong Liberal Democrat credentials scarcely made him an unbiased authority. Nor did he fully appreciate, at that time, the full nature and extent of the letters.

When he came to write an introduction to Violet's diaries and letters (*Lantern Slides*) in 1995, he seems to have changed his mind. He wrote: "The news, fifty years late, that Venetia exchanged even more frequent and more intimate letters and perhaps other intimacies as well, with her (Violet's) father, was therefore a natural and profound shock, for which I did not fully allow at the time (i.e. 1978). Compared with today, when the existence of even the most minor and boring scandals is shrieked out from every tabloid, pre 1914 England, was full of hidden sexual reefs."[128]

There can be no question, well-evidenced in their correspondence, but that Venetia did give Asquith much needed support. On 1 August 1914, for instance, he wrote: "All these days – full of incident and for the most part anxious and worrying – I have been sustained by the thought that when today came, I should once more see your darling face & be with you, and share everything and get from you what I value most, & what is to me the best of all things in the world – your counsel & your understanding & your sympathy and your love.… I should be desolate, if it were not for your sweetest of all letters this morning – the best, if not quite the best, that you have ever sent me – which gives me a new fund of courage and hope. My darling – can I ever thank you enough? Without you I tremble to think what wd have happened to me."

---

126 Jenkins, 258.

127 Jenkins, Introduction to 1978 edition.

128 *Lantern Slides*, xxviii.

In May 1915, Violet had recorded in her diary: "Poor darling [Asquith] said 'I have sometimes walked up and down that room till I felt as tho' I were going mad. When one needed rest, to have a thing, like the Morning Post, flung at one – all the obvious reasons for and against things, more controversially put even than by one's colleagues. Venetia rested him from all this."[129] But the fact that he was greatly dependent on her for advice and support is not inconsistent with their being lovers in the physical sense. Indeed, it may be thought to support the view.

In addition to the inferences to be drawn from the various strands, there is also the evidence of a number of witnesses, albeit some of it contradictory, which casts light on the relationship. Diana (later Diana Cooper), was one of the smart set and part of the Coterie. (She also had a meteoric stage career.) Reportedly, she told the Brocks that Venetia had told her that she, Venetia, was a virgin on her wedding night in July 1915.[130] However, Diana had been of the view in May 1915 that Venetia had been Asquith's mistress, and she confirmed this view in February 1984, when she told Angela Lambert that she believed that the "Asquith–Venetia relationship 'must' have included some sexual contact."[131] Angela was an authoress and journalist who wrote several books, among them the 1987 work, *Unquiet Souls: A Social History of the Illustrious, Irreverent, Intimate Group of British Aristocrats Known As "the Souls"*.

Margot's view about Asquith's relations with women is clear. She claimed not to be jealous of "his little harem", observing that "she welcomed them, as they fitted the theory which I have always held about wives – No woman should expect to be the only woman in her husband's life."[132] However in April 1915 she wrote " I feel terribly depressed and worried over a trifling domestic discouragement which

---

129 *Champion Redoubtable*, 55.
130 Levine, 234.
131 A.J.P. Taylor (Article in London Review of Books, 29 December 1982), 25.
132 Margot Asquith, *Off the Record* (Frederick Muller, London 1943), 122.

has baffled and bothered me for a long, long time" [133] In 1915, Asquith visited Diana when she happened to be in bed, still recovering from an accident. He made evident his distress at Venetia's desertion and his affection for Diana. Next day a letter arrived for her from Asquith, prominently marked "personal", with the instruction that any reply should be similarly labelled. Somewhat daunted by the letter's contents, that evening Diana consulted Duff Cooper, who was then her lover and subsequently her husband. He became a famous politician and was British Ambassador in Paris after the Second World War. In his diary for 20 July 1915, he wrote:

> "Went to Diana [Manners]. She was very intrigued by a letter she had had from the Prime Minister [Asquith] He had been to see her the other day and they had discussed at length Venetia's marriage. Diana is quite certain that Venetia was his mistress, which rather surprises me. This letter, which was rather obscurely expressed, seemed practically to be an offer to Diana to fill the vacated situation. She was in great difficulty as to how she was to answer it, partly from being uncertain as to its meaning, partly from the nature of the proposal which it seemed to contain. She was anxious not to lose him, but did not aspire to the position of his Egeria [i.e. counsellor] which she felt sure would entail physical duties that she couldn't or wouldn't fulfil. I advised her to concoct an answer which should be as obscure as his proposal and leave him puzzled – the old lecher."[134]

Diana's description of this visit omits any reference to the letter or proposition.[135] Diana also recorded that when she was 17, Asquith

---

133 Brocks .*Margot Asquith's Great War Diary* (OUP.2014) p.94

134 Norwich, 13. Ziegler, 76.

135 *The Rainbow Comes and Goes*, 140.

THE PRIME MINISTER AND HIS MISTRESS

used to want to hold her hand.[136] Duff further said of Asquith, "He is oblivious of young men and lecherous to young women."[137] This was a common view.

On another occasion, on the way back from a dinner party where she, Duff, and Asquith had all been, Asquith was determined to be alone with Diana in his car. Duff left the car and ran all the way across the park to ensure Diana's safe arrival at their house.[138]

A number of critics, in their reviews of Brock's book, wrote that in their opinion, there was no physical intimacy between Asquith and Venetia.[139] Peter Clarke, a professor of modern history at the University of Cambridge and the author of a number of distinguished books, wrote: "What Asquith seems to have done was to sublimate political tension into sexual fantasy, finding the release which was impossible with Margot in his ejaculations for Venetia."[140]

Ted Morgan, born Comte St Charles Armand de Gramont, is a journalist and author. He became an American citizen and changed his name to Morgan. He has won a number of prestigious literary awards, including a Pulitzer Prize. Among his political biographies is *Churchill: Young Man in a Hurry, 1874–1915*, wherein he described Venetia thus: "She said she was a pagan, she had no sense of sin, no penitential moods, no waves of remorse." Nevertheless, Morgan asserted that "his [Asquith's] love was never consummated, for Venetia was repelled by his drooling thigh-stroking advances: for the sixty-three year old Asquith, physical fulfilment was less important than the emotional comfort Venetia provided in her letters." The reference in support of this unequivocal view is given as "a confidential source."[141] The identity

---

136 Ibid. 105.

137 Ziegler, 77.

138 Norwich, 36.

139 Levine, i. 233–234.

140 Peter Clarke, *The Times Higher Educational Supplement* (London, 14 December 1983), 13.

141 Morgan, 519.

of the informant is not vouchsafed. In 1982, when Morgan's book was published, Asquith had been dead for fifty-four years, Venetia for thirty-four years, and Violet for thirteen years. Diana was still alive and is the most likely source. But if so, why was it necessary, after all the years which had now passed, for there to be any confidentiality?

Stephen Koss was an American historian specialising in Britain. He was a professor of history at Columbia University in New York and a visiting fellow of All Souls College, Oxford. His most famous books are two volumes written in 1981 and 1984 (and published as one volume) titled, *The Rise and Fall of Political Press in Britain*. Koss takes a more cynical view of the relationship between Asquith and Venetia. He wrote, "Were they lovers? More than one authority has casually identified her as his mistress", though he doesn't say who the authorities are. He adds: "His passionate declarations and tender endearments would tend to support such an interpretation."[142]

In her book *Unquiet Souls*, Angela Lambert, a close friend of both Asquith and Venetia, wrote, "Asquith had not the temperament for unconsummated love – certainly not platonic love. He was too full blooded to be a Balfour, palely loitering, especially as Margot became disinclined for sex after twenty years of marriage. As women soon found out, to be left alone with him was to invite immediate and bold approaches, admittedly playful to begin with, for hand holding, touching, fondling and kissing. He was simply, an importunate lecher – if he found no resistance to his advances – or even active encouragement – he would take the relationship to its fullest conclusion."[143] Lady Churchill disliked Asquith's predilection for peering down "Pennsylvania Avenue" (the contemporary expression for a lady's cleavage) whenever he was seated next to a pretty woman.[144] Diana complained of having to defend her face from "his fumbly

---

142 Stephen Koss, *Asquith* (London: Allen Lane, 1976), 140.

143 Lambert, 207.

144 Soames, 118.

hands and mouth."¹⁴⁵ Asquith himself wrote to Venetia, "I am fresh from the healing life-giving touch of your beloved hands." Stephen Bates, a journalist on the *Guardian,* suggests he was something of a groper,¹⁴⁶ and cites the view of Lytton Strachey, who had founded the Bloomsbury group and was a distinguished biographer, writing *The Eminent Victorians* in 1918.¹⁴⁷

A.J.P. Taylor was a controversial historian whose revisionist book *The Origins of the Second World War* caused a storm of protest when it was published. He was a prolific author, journalist and broadcaster. After a fellowship at Magdalen College, Oxford, he became a lecturer at the Institute of Historical Research at University College, London. He initially agreed with the view of Brock until he came across one of Asquith's letters, ending "You know how I long to …" Taylor observed "Now what are we to make of that – merely that Asquith wanted to hold Venetia's hand under the carriage rug? I doubt it."¹⁴⁸

According to Naomi Levine, the author of *Politics, Religion and Love* [The Story of H.H. Asquith, Venetia Stanley, and Edwin Montagu], Alistair Forbes, a long-time friend of Venetia and Diana, wrote to the *Times* that Diana did not suspect that Venetia was Asquith's mistress at the time, and "the account which Venetia gave Diana of her disagreeable brutal defloration to which she was subjected by her husband on her wedding night, could scarcely have caused her to change her opinion."¹⁴⁹ Unfortunately, the reference is totally inaccurate.¹⁵⁰ And Diana's

---

145 Artemis Cooper, 85.

146 Stephen Bates, *Asquith* (London: Haus Publishing), 73–74.

147 Clifford, 207.

148 Taylor, 25.

149 Levine, 234. The author notes the date of the letter to the *Times* as 14 December 1982 (p. 759, note 70), but the *Times* reports that there is no trace of such a letter of that date or any other date in its cutting files, on microfilm, or in its online archives. Lee Chilvers email, 5/4/11.

150 Ibid.

evidence is so contradictory as to be worthless. Nor do other arguments carry any more weight.

Colin Clifford was a journalist who had been economics correspondent for *The Sunday Times*. He wrote, "The morals of the time made such a relationship almost unthinkable for a young unmarried woman from the upper or middle classes. In any case, the opportunities for illicit sex would have been few and far between; continual entertaining; and, ever present servants, would have ensured that the couple were rarely alone."[151]

This is manifest nonsense, as can be seen from four well-known examples. Though he was married, Lloyd George managed to have a longstanding affair with Frances Stevenson.[152] Grey, later the foreign secretary, started a love affair with Pamela Tennant while he was married. She was the widow of Lord Glenconner and later was married to Eddy Tennant, Margot's brother. The relationship between Grey and Pamela lasted for many years, and they eventually married in 1922. It appears that Grey had probably been the father of Pamela's fourth child, David, born many years earlier.[153] Grey may also have had an affair with Florence Slee, who bore him a daughter, Winifred.[154] It is thought that in 1911 Grey may also have been the father of Janet Lincoln, who was adopted by a well-to-do family in Massachusetts.[155] Venetia may not have been the daughter of Lord Sheffield,[156] and Diana's father was certainly not the Duke of Rutland, but Harry Cust, a brilliant Old Etonian, who became an MP in 1890. The Duchess of Rutland, Diana's mother, was not his only conquest.[157]

Therefore, what the correspondence and other examples make

---

151 Clifford, 207.

152 Frances Stevenson, passim.

153 Michael Waterhouse, *Edwardian Requiem: A Life of Sir Edward Grey* (London: Biteback Publishing Ltd., 2013), 95.

154 Ibid. 43–48.

155 Ibid. 256–257.

156 Notes, 45–46.

157 Clifford, 33 n. Ziegler, 16, 39.

abundantly clear is that there was ample opportunity for illicit sex which the absence of an intrusive press facilitated. Nor is there any reason to believe that morals in the 1910s, among all classes, were any different from those of any other generation.

Philip Ziegler, the well-known author of a number of political biographies, wrote:

> Marital fidelity was not a virtue highly esteemed among the British aristocracy. Many husbands kept women on the side: once the wife had produced an heir, she often felt that her work was done and she could now relax. The only requirement was that one should not be caught out; in Mrs Patrick Campbell's no doubt apocryphal phrase: "It doesn't matter what you do in the bedroom as long as you don't do it in the street and frighten the horses."[158]

Clifford wrote: "Lytton Strachey revealed in an essay ... how Lady Otteline Morrell, an English aristocrat and society hostess – had told him how Asquith 'would take a lady's hand, as she sat on the sofa, and make him feel his erected instrument under his trousers.'"[159] "The notoriously scandal-mongering Strachey," wrote Clifford, "is not the most reliable source but in this case it rings true."[160]

Another reference, again from Levine, states that a Nicholas Walter wrote this letter to the *Times* in 1983:

> "My father, W. Grey Walter, who was one of Venetia Montagu's young lovers fifty years ago ... (and I inherited the Cartier cigarette case he was given for services rendered) told me in the 1970's that she told

---

158 Ziegler, 14.

159 Beauman, 195. Michael Holroyd and Paul Levy, eds., *The Shorter Strachey* (OUP Oxford, 1980), 38–42.

160 Clifford, 207.

him in the 1930's, that Asquith had been her lover in the full sense in the 1910's..."[161]

At first sight this seems pretty conclusive evidence, but this reference, unfortunately, is also totally inaccurate.[162]

It is quite true that Asquith wrote many passionate letters to other girlfriends. After Venetia married, Asquith corresponded with her sister Sylvia Henley, to whom he wrote some 390 letters between 1915 and 1919. Others to whom he often wrote included Lady Scott, Mrs Harrisson, Pamela Jekyll, Viola Tree, Dorothy Beresford, and Margot's niece Lilian Tennant, but it was to Venetia (or as Margot described her in 1909, "Violet's Squaw") that he devoted his attentions almost exclusively from 1912 until May 1915. In 1916, Venetia had what was described as an "Aaron's operation", a procedure to facilitate intercourse and make it easier for her to carry out her marital (or extramarital) obligations.[163] Given that she had by then been married for a year to Edwin, this information throws no light on her relationship with Asquith. In January 1919, she referred to the operation again, telling Montagu that she was going to have an Aaron's operation to "take care of a little thing wrong with me."[164]

In seeking to answer the question of their relationship, it is therefore also necessary to look at any evidence other than direct evidence which happens to be available. In family law, courts have always been able to come to the conclusion that parties have been guilty of adultery even without there being direct evidence.

---

161 Levine, 234–235. The author notes the date of the letter to the *Times* as 7 January 1983 (p. 759, note 72), but the *Times* reports that it has no trace of such a letter in its cutting files, on microfilm, or in its online archive. Lee Chilvers email, 5/4/11. The only letter from a Nicholas Walter to the *Times* between January 1967 and December 1985 is dated 23 November 1979, and relates to Blunt.

162 Ibid.

163 Cynthia Asquith, 238.

164 MG, Jan 30 1919.

"The fact of adultery may be inferred from circumstances which by fair inference lead to that necessary conclusion. There must be proof of disposition or inclination and opportunity for committing adultery, but the conjunction of strong inclination with evidence of opportunity does not lead to an *irrebuttable*[165] presumption that adultery has been committed, nor is the Court bound to infer adultery from opportunity alone."[166]

In *Allen v Allen,* Lopes, L.J. added these observations: "To lay down any general rule, to attempt to define what circumstances would be sufficient and what would be insufficient upon which to infer the fact of adultery is impossible ... A jury in a case like the present ought to exercise their judgement ... applying their knowledge of the world and of human nature ... and then determine whether those circumstances are capable of any other reasonable solution than that of the guilt of the party, sought to be implicated."[167]

In *Ross v Ellison or Ross*, Lord Atkin said, "But from opportunities alone no inference of misconduct can fairly be drawn unless the conduct of the parties, prior, contemporaneous, or subsequent, justifies the inference that such feelings existed between the parties that opportunities, if given, would be used for misconduct."

The direct evidence from witnesses is contradictory, and no firm conclusions can be drawn from them. There is, in modern parlance, no smoking gun among the letters constituting direct evidence, though not all his letters are extant and hers are almost non-existent. It is necessary, therefore, to try and draw inferences.

Asquith's descriptions of Venetia in *Portraits of a Lady* scarcely describe a femme fatale or a girl consumed by wild passion for an

---

[165] Italics mine.

[166] *Halsbury's Laws of England,* 5th edition, lxxii. par. 353.

[167] 1894, Probate Reports, 251 at 254.

older man. Indeed, Violet told Jenkins that she could not believe her father had had a special relationship with Venetia "because she was so plain."[168] Finally, it has to be remembered that these were essentially private letters which he was writing to Venetia, in which it might be expected that a lover would at least have made some passing reference to their lovemaking, if it had in fact occurred. Nowhere, in the available correspondence is such a direct reference to be found, though some of the language used might readily lead to that conclusion. Thus, if such an inference is to be drawn, it must depend on six separate strands to the relationship which both individually and cumulatively lead to the conclusion that this was more than a platonic affair.

Nor can the "aphrodisiac of power" be totally ignored. Politicians have always had affairs. Taylor suggests that Gladstone identified six previous prime ministers who had been adulterers.[169] There have been other politicians since. Lloyd George and Beaverbrook were not the first, nor indeed the last. It is not necessary to go very far back in history to record a litany of such affairs. Lloyd George and Beaverbrook were lucky to suffer no setback in their political careers, due no doubt to the ignorance of the popular press at the time. Others were not so lucky. Two contemporaries of Asquith suffered disaster to their political careers as a result of extramarital affairs. Perhaps it is no wonder that, as we shall see, the Asquiths have airbrushed Venetia from their memoirs.

The first, Sir Charles Dilke, became a Liberal MP in 1868. By December 1882, he was a member of Gladstone's cabinet as president of the local government board. He was a leading radical reformer and was already being spoken of as a future prime minister. In 1886, a fellow MP, Donald Crawford, brought divorce proceedings against his wife, Virginia, and against Dilke, alleging that they had committed adultery. The evidence was substantially based on a confession by Virginia. She declined to give evidence on oath. In the result, the judge decided that Virginia had indeed committed adultery with Dilke, but because she did

---

168 Pottle, xxv.

169 Taylor, 25.

not give evidence on oath, it was not evidence against Dilke, who was accordingly dismissed from the suit and awarded costs.

The case caused serious damage to Dilke's reputation. In order now to do something to clear his name, Dilke was advised to seek to reopen the case. In the event, Dilke's evidence was then subjected to a vigorous cross-examination by Henry Matthews, QC for Mrs Crawford, and destroyed. The jury found that Virginia's version was true, and a decree absolute was pronounced. In the 1886 general election, Dilke lost his parliamentary seat. He managed to find another seat in 1892, but his hopes of being appointed as secretary of state for war in the Liberal government of 1905 were not to be realised. His attempts to exonerate himself cost him much effort and time and much of his fortune to no effect. He became old and arid in his disappointment.[170]

Another of Asquith's contemporaries whose extramarital activities destroyed his reputation was Charles Parnell. In 1890, Parnell was about to reach the zenith of his powers. Gladstone described him as the most remarkable person he had ever met, and Asquith's view was that he was one of the three or four greatest men that he had ever met. In 1888 and 1889, he was in the process of negotiating the details of a new home rule bill with Gladstone on behalf of the Irish Party.

In December 1889, a Captain O'Shea filed for divorce against his wife, Kitty, on the ground of her adultery, citing Parnell as a co-respondent. Parnell and Kitty had been having an affair for a number of years, and he had fathered three of her children. The trial came on in November 1890. Parnell did not defend the proceedings. He lost the leadership of his party. Although Parnell fought a vigorous campaign for reinstatement, his failing health and the bitter opposition of his former associates ensured that he never again achieved success. The divorce, thus, was to have a disastrous effect on Irish politics, both at the time, and ever since. In October 1891, Parnell died.

In more modern times, a list of adulterous politicians would include, among others, John Major (prime minister of Great Britain), François

---

170 Roy Jenkins, *Sir Charles Dilke* (London: Collins, 1958), 214, passim.

Mitterand (president of France), Silvio Berlusconi (prime minister of Italy), Dwight Eisenhower, John Kennedy, William Clinton (presidents of the USA), Bob Hawke (prime minister of Australia), Robert Boothby, Chris Huhne, John Prescott, Robin Cook, and John Profumo (British Ministers). Profumo's career ended, not because of his affair with Christine Keeler, but because he lied to the House of Commons.

A well-respected political commentator described the pathology of the politician (the Aphrodisiac of power) in this way:

> "Elective office feeds your vanity and starves your self-respect. What then are the compensations that, for those who choose this life, make it all worthwhile? They are these. First, a craving for applause, for being a somebody, for being looked up to. The read-across from this to the sexual behaviour of middle–aged men in politics is too obvious to need stating; power is indeed an aphrodisiac; but for the powerful, for the predator rather than his prey, it is like having a big sports car.
>
> Second, a completely and persistently unrealistic belief in your own good luck.… Third – and this is truly weird – an awfully thin skin … all this leads to frequent pain, frequent euphoria, … an obsessive drive to keep asking for more until … something big and external to yourself – finally fells you."[171]

In June 1885, Dilke wrote to his mistress, Mrs Pattison, "It is in old age that power comes. It is possible for an old man in English politics to exert enormous power without effort, and with little call upon his time, and no drain upon his health and vital force.… It is in old age, only, that power can be used legitimately and peacefully by the once strong man."[172] Does this throw any light on Asquith's behaviour? For

---

171 Matthew Parris, *Spectator*, 21 May 2011, 13.
172 Dilke, Papers. British Museum D.P.43906,106.

the prey, too, there is the excitement of engaging in an illicit affair, of sharing state secrets, and of being privy to important decisions. How could Venetia not be overwhelmed by the flattery of a much older man's attention, or by the enormous prestige inherent in the relationship? Thus, for predator and prey alike, an affair makes perfect sense.

In the case of Asquith and Venetia, the six strands, which lawyers would identify as suggesting that the relationship was an adulterous one (in no particular order of importance), are as follows.

First, the subsequent behaviour of Venetia with a number of married men while still married to Montagu suggests a girl of few morals.

Second, the age and relative status of Asquith and Venetia, to which there has already been much reference.

Third, the language and volume of the correspondence.

Fourth, the private communication of highly confidential and secret information, not only before the war, but more importantly, during the war, and his frequent reliance on Venetia's advice about a number of sensitive decisions, both military and political. The correspondence bears all the hallmarks of a couple leading a conjugal life.

Fifth, in the various extensive memoirs of the Asquith family, there is what can only be described as a conspiracy of silence about the very existence of Venetia in Asquith's life. Collectively, the family have simply airbrushed Venetia out of their consciousness. The relationship was "the dog which didn't bark".

Sixth, there were the frequent arrangements for private meetings which would have provided ample opportunity for lovemaking.

CHAPTER SIX

Venetia's Subsequent Behaviour

Venetia's character is most clearly defined by her continued membership in the Corrupt Coterie and its successor and later, while she was still married to Montagu, by becoming the mistress of two and possibly more lovers. Her bedroom was described as "that of a courtesan".[173]

Her marriage to Montagu had been less than a great success. She had always found him physically unattractive. On one occasion she referred to him "as an old swine".[174] In August 1915, not long after the marriage, Cynthia found her in "the most extraordinary mood of apparent, complete ennui and lifelessness.... I am sure the marooned honeymoon, even if unpleasant, is really the most wholesome. It doesn't do to dodge the situation and each other by living in a crowd."[175]

Raymond, Asquith's son, wrote to a friend, "I understand that the terms of alliance permit a wide licence to both parties to indulge such extra-conjugal caprices as either may be lucky enough to conceive."[176]

In May 1918, Diana wrote:

---

173 Cynthia Asquith, 107.

174 Ibid. 98.

175 Ibid. 74.

176 John Jolliffe, *Raymond Asquith: Life and Letters* (London: Collins, 1980) 202.

"Alan [Parsons] told me that Venetia's letters [to Montagu] were so unbelievably dreadful that no one an inch less besotted with love than Edwin could have tolerated them. Beginning always with the worn gambit of "darling, I wrote you a frightfully good letter, but have already lost it, so must write another one, a bad one. Last night I dined with …" Then follows a long succession of dinners and their guests, without even a peroration of love: nothing in fact that Edwin could not give Alan to read."[177]

By June 1918, Diana was expressing a dismal view of the marriage, "opining that Venetia – having essentially 'married him for her days rather than her nights' – was now (after her interval of grass widowhood) tortured by real repugnance and that Edwin appeared plunged in gloom."[178]

Edwin was also at this time in serious financial difficulties and was looking to Beaverbrook to help pay £60,000 off his debts.[179] In August, Diana wrote to Duff that while she was at the Montagus' house at Breccles, Montagu had made advances to her, adding, "I think Venetia refuses him and he is half mad with desires. Poor baboon."[180] A few days later she wrote again, "the relationship of the Monts [Montagus] is worse daily … he had preceded us and was out shooting when we arrived, and returning in the middle of dinner … he kissed my hands first and then Viola's fervently, and in fond anticipation of Venetia's at last, but smilelessly she did not let it meet his lips and with an irritated gesture asked a gruff question about a bailiff. I am not magnifying and I am terrified."[181]

---

177 Cooper, *Artemis*, 57.
178 Ibid. 456.
179 Ibid. 76.
180 Ibid. 92–93.
181 Ibid. 95–96.

Duff's view of the marriage in November was much the same. He wrote: "The relations of Edwin and Venetia are very distressing. She seems hardly able to bear him – she cannot help showing it and he cannot help seeing it."[182] In April 1919, his diary records: "I find I am wrong in supposing Venetia and Edwin are happy. He confessed this evening to Diana that he has never been more miserable. Alas, I no longer like and cannot pity him.... He is a man incapable of inspiring trust, confidence or lasting love. He has great qualities of charm and intellect but they are all warped by something which I believe to be a mixture of cowardice, jealousy and suspicion."[183]

Friends did not feel that there was anything to be done about the marriage or in trying to put the Montagus right, as "they don't exist at all".[184]

Duff recorded another incident about Venetia's love affairs. In 1919 he wrote,

> "The conversation fell on reading other people's letters. Edwin told how he had once found, in a book addressed to Venetia, the most compromising letter he had ever read. He had written her, thereupon, a severe reproof, warning remonstrance, but then had changed his mind, thought his own letter too pompous and had destroyed both".[185]

History does not relate the name of the author of the letter nor its date. Given this rather unhappy picture, it is perhaps not surprising that Venetia took lovers. The two best known were Beaverbrook and the Earl of Dudley, though there were undoubtedly others.

The liaison with Beaverbrook probably first started in 1917. In 1919, Diana was in Paris for the Peace Conference with her mother. So

---

182 Norwich, 85.

183 Ibid. 97.

184 Ziegler, 75.

185 Norwich, 110.

too were Venetia and Montagu, together with Beaverbrook, who was without his wife. Diana wrote to Duff, "Crooks [i.e. Beaverbrook] and Venetia turned up just as we were turning out. Its a disgusting case ... her face lights up when that animated little deformity so much as turns to her. They are living in open sin at the Ritz in a tall silk suite, with a common bath, and unlocked doors between, while poor Ted [Edwin] is sardined into the Majestic, unknown and uncared for."[186]

When Diana visited Venetia at the Ritz, "she could hear Crooks's ablutions next door." On one occasion, after they had all dined together, Diana wrote, "I've just left Crooks and V in their luxurious nest and expedited Ted [Montagu] to his Etoille."[187]

Of a suggestion that Venetia should go to the South of France for a holiday on her own, Diana wrote to Duff, "I spoke to Edwin seriously about the desirability [of a holiday for Venetia] and he, against all expectation encourages it. I think he is mad keen to get rid of Venetia ... who he undoubtedly loves less daily. He said she had not been happy for three years ... and that she might be so there ... he became petitionary. Looks bad baby."[188]

Venetia had supplied Beaverbrook with some of Asquith's letters and helped him with his account of Asquith's fall in 1916. She further provided him with very useful information about the progress of the Peace Conference. They regularly went out together in Paris, and he visited her at the Montagus' house at Breccles. Even when Montagu was ill in a nursing home in 1920, she and Beaverbrook arranged to meet regularly. When Beaverbrook's wife died in 1927, he turned in despair to Venetia and she gave him comfort.[189] Although he had other mistresses, he and Venetia kept up a passionate correspondence until her death in 1948. He showered presents and money on her at regular intervals and helped her with her investments.

---

186 Cooper, *Artemis*, 131.

187 Ibid. 131–132.

188 Ibid. 133.

189 Ann Chisholm and Michael Davie, *Beaverbrook. A Life* (London: Hutchinson Publishing Co. Ltd., 1992), 261.

Beaverbrook was not Venetia's only lover. Eric Ednam, later the third Earl of Dudley, was another. He was probably the father of Venetia's daughter, Judith (known as Judy). Eric's wife, whom he married in 1943, wrote in her autobiography, "I was fond of Venetia, who was not only a contemporary of Eric's, but had had a love affair with him years before, which had resulted in a child, Judy Montagu, who was a great friend of mine."[190] Judy's daughter, Anna, confirmed that her mother had told her that she, Judy, was the child of Venetia and Dudley.[191] Perhaps in those circumstances it is not very surprising that Venetia concealed from Montagu the date when the baby [Judy] was due.[192]

Other names rumoured to be Venetia's lovers were Sir Matthew "Scatters" Wilson and Charles Hope. The former was the prototype of the Edwardian rake, described in 1917 as "a funny, ebullient bounder, with his blue eyes and hoarse whisper."[193]

The rumours about her association with Scatters were widespread. Cynthia recorded in July 1918, "I liked Scatters. He ... drove me home. Either the scandal as to him and Venetia is – as I believe – purely legendary, or he is the most consummate misleader, because we discussed Venetia in the taxi and he diagnosed her as a jolly 'Long haired chum' not 'out for a fling' ... and quite out of the siren class.... But, I can't understand Venetia's strange burst of beauty."[194]

Another of Venetia's friends was Sidney Herbert, who was Duff's best man. Of him, Duff recorded in September 1919, "Sidney and Venetia dined with us.... Venetia and Sidney are very much together, now Edwin is away at Breccles whither Venetia returns tomorrow."[195]

Her adultery with a number of lovers while still married to Montagu

---

190 Duchess of Marlborough, *Laughter from a Cloud* (London: Weidefeld and Nicolson, 1980), 111.

191 Levine, 670–673.

192 Norwich, 175.

193 Cynthia Asquith, 300.

194 Cynthia Asquith, 460.

195 Norwich, 108.

may shed some light on her relationship with Asquith, by reference to a doctrine in criminal law known as *propensity*. What that means in very general terms (and it is based on common sense) is that if it can be shown that an accused had a propensity or (in non-legal language) the inclination to commit particular offences, evidence of that propensity may be adduced if he is subsequently charged with a similar offence. His previous history will make it more likely that he is in fact guilty of the subsequent offence.[196] Strictly, propensity relates to *previous* and not *subsequent* behaviour. However, in *R v Adinusi*, the court of appeal (criminal division) held that conduct, subsequent to the allegation, the subject matter of the trial, was admissible. Lord Justice Hooper said, "We can see no justification for saying that, as a matter of law, one is not entitled to determine propensity at the time of committing the offence by reference to offences committed thereafter."[197]

Is it in any way unreasonable to ask as a matter of common sense why, if Venetia were willing to ignore her husband and have a number of lovers when she was a *married* woman, it should be thought surprising that she should have had a sexual relationship with Asquith only a few years earlier, when she was *single* and not constrained by the ties of marriage?

---

196 Ss 101–103 Criminal Justice Act 2003.

197 2006 EWCA. Crim. 1059 at par. 13.

CHAPTER SEVEN

The Language and Volume of the Correspondence

While some of Asquith's letters to Venetia contain classical allusions, political confidences, and references to social events, they are above all written in the most passionate and amorous manner. He would often start "My darling", "My dearly beloved", "Thank you my darling for you delicious letter", and "Most dear". Her frequent letters were often described as "delicious", and he made no secret of the fact that he was hopelessly in love with her.

His letters are full of passion and entreaties of love. Extracts from different letters read: "The Great men have come and gone – and all the time I *longed* for you to be here." "Yours through life – always – everywhere." "Most dear – never more dear – I love you with heart and soul." "All I know is that I am (whatever you may ever be) always – everywhere – wholly yours." " I am carrying about with me in my pocket the most delicious letter you have ever sent me. Nothing for years has given me such intense pleasure as your assurance that you don't want me *ever* to stop loving you and wanting you." "My precious darling.... You are always with me, nearer and dearer every day. Your *own* ..." "There is nothing else in the world that I would put in comparison with it (your praise) Your *own* – in *life* & till death." "My love for you has grown day by day & month by month & (now) year by year till it absorbs and inspires all my life. I could not if I would, and I would not if I could, arrest its flow or limit its extent or lower by a single degree its intensity, or make it a less sovereign & dominating factor in my thoughts and purposes and hopes. It has rescued me (little as anyone but you know it) from sterility, impotence, despair. It enables me in the daily stress of almost intolerable burdens & anxieties to see visions and dream dreams."

On 8 March 1915, while he was writing this last letter from the House of Commons, saying that his love for Venetia was "absorbing all his life", the war and its conduct was about to take a dramatic turn. Two particular events dominated the political horizon – as Asquith confessed to Venetia. The first was the failure of the naval attempt to force the Dardanelles, and the second was the debate over the shortage of ammunition.

The first idea for breaking the stalemate on the Western Front was suggested by Churchill, then first lord of the admiralty, in December 1914. The proposal was to invade Schleswig Holstein. This would have the effect of threatening the Kiel Canal and possibly inducing Denmark to enter the war on the side of the Allies. In that event, the fleet would have command of the Baltic, and the Russians would be enabled more easily to attack the Germans. It did not take long for the feasibility of this scheme to be rejected.

The next idea (conceived by Lloyd George) was to send troops to the Balkans to support Serbia and thus to encourage Greece, Romania, and Bulgaria to enter the war on the Allies' side. It would also threaten Austria and Turkey. This plan, too, was rejected.

The Westerners argued that only in the West could Germany be defeated and that any reduction in the numbers of troops there would seriously threaten the safety of France. The French themselves were opposed to any idea of withdrawing troops from the Western Front, more particularly with German soldiers on the soil of France. They also pointed out the difficulties of transporting large numbers of troops by sea. When the council met on 13 January, the Westerners won the day, supported – unsurprisingly – by French.

But Churchill was not to be discouraged from his Dardanelles scheme. He now proposed that the exercise should be carried out substantially as a naval operation. Battleships were to be sent to destroy the Turkish forts on the shore. Thereafter, once the straits had been cleared of any mines, the way would be clear for the ships to sail to Constantinople, thereby putting Turkey out of the war. On 28 January, the scheme, as a purely naval operation, was approved.

But the "purely naval operation" turned into a massive combined military and naval operation, because the navy had failed to silence the Turkish guns on shore or to force their way up the straits. On 19 February, the naval bombardment had begun, but further operations were then delayed by bad weather until 25 February. On 2 March, it was now thought that a fortnight would be necessary to force the straits.

There were serious problems. There was a shortage of minesweepers, the channels were narrow, and the current was swift. And there were two other unforeseen difficulties. While the permanent forts could be identified and destroyed, the Turks used mobile batteries, which were difficult to locate. Additionally, the channel was now sown with complicated and constantly renewed minefields.

On 8 March, three battleships struck mines laid by the Turks and sank. The attempt by the navy to force the straits was called off. Kitchener decided that it was safe for the Twenty-Ninth Division to proceed to Lemnos, from where, with other forces, it was to seize Gallipoli. The expedition would end in disaster.

The ammunition crisis which arose a few weeks later led to the formation of a coalition government and eventually to Asquith's replacement as prime minister in December 1916. There had been growing criticism of the stalemate in France. The strategy appeared flawed, the military intelligence almost worthless, and the gains achieved minimal. The belief that the casualties were due to a shell shortage gradually grew strength. A Munitions Committee had been appointed in 1914, but met only six times before it was abandoned in January 1915. One of the problems was that Kitchener did not approve of any civilian interference in matters which he regarded as a purely military issue.

On 6 March, Asquith had written to Venetia, "So far as things at home are concerned, the thorniest question is how is one to get more labour and plant for making armaments and other things needed for the war." The labour problem was that a lot of the skilled armament workers had joined Kitchener's army, and their replacements were unskilled or semiskilled men and women. Output had fallen seriously. Asquith continued, "I think we will have to 'take over' the principal firm, leaving the management in its present hands, but keeping the whole business especially the division of profits during the war, the distribution of work & of labour, and the wages to be paid to the workmen, under government supervision."

The letter of 8 March 1915 was by no means the only occasion when he confessed how much of his time was absorbed by his love for Venetia. On 25 July 1914, he had written, "Every hour I think of you & refer things big and little to the unseen tribunal of your wise and loving judgement." On 24 March 1915, he wrote, "I wonder if you can realise how at *every* hour of the day I am thinking of you." On 30 March he wrote, "In every crisis in my life, the thought and love of you dominates everything else."

From the outbreak of war in August 1914 until Venetia's engagement in May 1915, a period of less than ten months, Asquith wrote some 352 letters to her. In three highly critical months of the war, between mid February and mid May 1915, he managed to find time to write some 125 letters to Venetia. There were days when he wrote twice. Occasionally he wrote three times, and on one occasion four times in a day. On 19 February 1915, he observed: "Darling – it was more sweet than I can tell you to be assured that what I pour in upon you –three letters in the day – is welcome & does *something* to enrich your life. I shall go on – always – till you tell me – if you ever do – that you have had enough." On 5 March, "Four letters in one day! It is almost incredible, but I warn you it may happen again." It did.

While her letters to him were probably less numerous, they were by no means infrequent, as his constant description of "her delicious letters" makes clear. Apart from spending a lot of his time writing to Venetia, Asquith also seems to have spent an inordinate amount of time reading and rereading the letters which she had written to him. On 29 September 1914, he wrote, "My darling – you will never guess how many times I have read over and over (on a very busy day) your precious letter of this morning." On 30 October, "My darling – a delicious letter from you this morning.... I keep everyone and you don't know & couldn't guess how many times each is read in the course of 24 hours." On 2 November (at midnight), "My darling – I have been reading over again (for how many times do you think?) your dear letter of today ..." On 24 January 1915, again, "Your two letters of Fr & Sat arrived side by side by the morning post. They have already been read many times...."

Conducting government business both before and during the war was not allowed to interfere with Asquith's letters to Venetia. On 27 January 1914, he wrote, "And now as I am writing, we are in the full stress of Cabinet discussion." On 8 July, he wrote, "We had a long and rather dreary Cabinet this morning.... I am writing from the House, where we are still debating this tiresome guillotine." On 4 September (the war was now a month old), he wrote, "I am writing this at the Cabinet & have to be careful.... I got back here in time for the Cabinet wh is just over." On 30 December he wrote, *"very secret* ... perhaps I may be able to squeeze in a line or two while the Cabinet is sitting." On 13 January 1915, he told Venetia, "we are now [4 p.m.] in the midst of our War Council, wh began at 12, adjourned at 2, & is now sitting again.... a most interesting discussion.... *Later.* The Council is now over, having arrived harmoniously at 4 conclusions suggested by me." On 27 January, he was again writing, "I have been presiding this afternoon – as the earlier sheets of my letter show – at the Committee of Defence. It is what is called a full meeting.... they had a long discussion in which I took very little part.... in the end I formulated 2 or 3 rather platitudinous propositions to wh. they all agreed. In the intervals I began this letter to you." When he wrote the first "Portrait of a Lady", it was done "in the interludes of the Cabinet and the House." On 11 and 15 February, two letters, in the build-up to the unsuccessful attempt on the Dardanelles, were written while on the treasury bench.

On 25 February, he continued to confide news of Cabinet discussions "in this the Cabinet room. A most animated wrangle is in progress as to the conditions of price, qualities etc under which the Indian Government are to be allowed to export the surplus of their wheat crop.... I am a more or less detached spectator, occasionally throwing in a question which sets them all by the ears." On 22 March, he discussed more Cabinet secrets with her: "my own darling – I am writing in the stress and tumult of a windy and wordy controversy about munitions &c between Ll.G[eorge], Winston & A.J.B[alfour] ... and I daren't abstract myself more." On 15 April, he found another subject to interest Venetia. "My darling – I am sitting in the Cabinet room at a really interesting Committee ... on the great Drink Problem. I have never before attended a meeting of this particular Committee."

On 19 April, the day after the naval attack on the Dardanelles forts was called off, Asquith lost no time in telling Venetia of other Cabinet discussions. "I am writing this in Cabinet, where we are at present discussing in a rather desultory way, Italy, Greece, Bulgaria etc etc.... we are now in the thick of an animated tho. not as yet intemperate discussion of the great problem of drink.... *Later.* (1/4 to 6) The Cabinet is now over & will add a line before post time..."

On the same day, Montagu was also writing to Venetia, "I am not the only member of the Cabinet writing to you during its deliberations"

Asquith continued to fill his spare time at the House of Commons by writing to Venetia. On 22 April he confided, "I am writing this at the House between my questions & having to go in to pay tribute to the Sergeant at Arms (!) & to listen to Jack Tennant & Walter Long. I will try & add something on the bench. *Later* – we have all paid our little *eloges* to the expiring Sergeant at Arms."

Morgan gives a graphic description of these events. "A messenger would come into the Cabinet room with a letter from Venetia and he [Asquith] would read it with great concentration and then settle down to reply at length, ringing for the messenger, who would then take the reply for dispatch. Other members of the Cabinet, particularly Lloyd George, were dismayed at the time he spent on his personal correspondence, during meetings over which he should have been presiding, lost in his private thoughts, while grave wartime matters were being discussed."[198]

---

198 Ted Morgan, *Churchill: Young Man in a Hurry, 1874–1915.* (New York: Simon & Schuster, Inc., 1982) 519.

He ended his letters in a passionate way. "Dearest love Always." "All my love." "I so much want and need to see you again, beloved" "Bless you – all my love." "Goodnight my sweetest and best." "Goodnight dearly beloved. I hope I may dream of you." "Take care of yourself, darling – all love." "I need thy presence every passing hour. All my love." "If you were only nearer! – but near or far, you are my beloved & fill my heart &thoughts" "You will think of me tomorrow, darling won't you? and I shall have your white heather very near my heart.... All my love always." "Most dear and precious – your love is my life." "You are always with me, nearer and dearer every day. Your *own*." "All that I do and try to do, I do with the hope of earning your praise. There is nothing in the world that I would put in comparison with it. Your *own – in life & till death*." "You are the breath of my life, and the last words of my 1st Sonnet ('Strong in Thy strength, I live because I love') are the *literal truth*." "Most precious, you are all the light of all my days – the love and glory of my life. Your own." "And I shall live on the thought of what you have been & are to me and of what you are *in yourself* – the one incarnation of all that I worship. Your *lover – for all time*.... And above all, & beyond all, in the intimacy of perfect confidence & understanding, for 2 years past, the pole-star & lode-star of my life."

The passionate nature of their relationship and the length of it, as exemplified by the whole of their correspondence, tends to give support to the view that this was no passing phase of calf love between lovelorn teenagers, but expressions only consistent with an adulterous relationship.

CHAPTER EIGHT

Confidential Information and Advice

The constant exchange of highly confidential information between Asquith and Venetia and the reliance which he placed on her advice and opinions on a wide variety of topics further tend to suggest a relationship akin to a normal married couple who share all their intimate secrets with each other and with no one else. Even before the war, there were many sensitive political issues which Asquith shared with her and on which he sought (and received) her advice. This he frequently adopted as his own. Asquith wrote it is important "to have someone from whom you have no secrets, and upon whose understanding, judgement and love, you can implicitly rely".

During the war, he expressed his gratitude for her advice when in January 1915 he told her:

> "You know how I value your judgement. I put it *quite* first among women, and there are only 2 or 3 men to my mind, in the same class. And you have now shared my inmost confidence so long & and with such unsurpassing loyalty, that I can speak to you really *more freely* about the most important things, than I can to any other human being. It is a wonderful, & I believe, a unique relationship. Of course, now that you are hustled for time, you can't write much about these things, tho. I hope you will give your view whenever you can."

A week earlier he had confided, "I wanted so much, at the earliest opportunity, and while the impressions were still fresh, to talk to you & get your opinions about today's War Council."

One particular habit of Asquith's has given rise to serious criticism. He seems to have had no qualms at all about forwarding to Venetia for her information and advice private letters and despatches which he had personally received, without either the consent or even the knowledge of the author. On 13 April 1915, the *Times* had published a leading article strongly critical of the shortage of ammunition.[199] Asquith, in forwarding to Venetia a private letter he had received from Kitchener, added: "It [Kitchener's letter] shows how wicked was the lie invented by the *Times* yesterday that our lack of ammunition at the front was holding back, not only our own Army, but the French. Of course you won't breathe a word of it." On 14 April a second Munitions Committee was formed with Lloyd George as chairman. On the same day, Kitchener reported to Asquith, "I have had a talk with French. He told me he could let you know that with the present supply of ammunition, he will have as much as his troops will be able to use on the next forward movement." But on the same day, French was reported as saying, "I know what we want and must have, and that is more and more ammunitions."[200]

Asquith enclosed Kitchener's letter to Venetia. "I send you – *to keep secret or destroy*, as you think best, a letter I got about noon from K[itchener] recording the result of his private interview this morning with Sir J. French." On another occasion he was able to write, "I must send you the enclosed despatch of E. Grey's. It shows the kind of almost school-boy simplicity, both of mind and speech which is intertwined with great qualities."

A constant topic before the war in the correspondence between Asquith and Venetia related to the problems of the Aberdeens. By 1914, given the political situation in Ireland, the post of lord lieutenant there (effectively as governor) had acquired great significance. Lord Aberdeen

---

199 *Times*, 13 April, 1915, 9.

200 *Times*, 13 April 1915, 8.

had held the post since 1906 and had now served his time. Two questions immediately arose. The first related to the date when he (and more particularly Lady Aberdeen) could be persuaded to leave, and the second was who should be appointed as his successor. In March 1914, Asquith told Venetia that he had had a discussion with Birrell, the chief secretary for Ireland about the succession, and that Birrell was rather in favour of Lord Lucas as Aberdeen's successor.[201]

On 27 July, Asquith told Venetia, "The state of things in Dublin is still far from agreeable and I am tempted to regret that I didn't take the clean cut, 6 months ago, and insist on the booting out of Aberdeen … & the whole crew. A weaker and more incompetent lot were never in charge of a leaky ship, in stormy weather …"

In September, Asquith was still canvassing Venetia's view about candidates to replace Aberdeen. "In regard to Ireland and the succession to the Aberdeens, they, Montagu and Eric Drummond [one of Asquith's Private Secretaries], were both anti Wimborne and anti Dick Cavendish, and strongly in favour of the Gladstones. Tell me what you think about this; you know that your judgement comes first with me." Wimborne did not have Venetia's approval.

In October, Asquith told Aberdeen that he had been in post for nearly nine years and that it was now time for him to retire. This generated much heated correspondence, both from Aberdeen himself and from Lady Aberdeen, as Asquith reported to Venetia on 10 October. "I have had poor Aberdeen's reply to my letter this morning; it covers 7 quarto pages."

Violet had an even more poignant appeal from Lady A: "How can your Father wreak such havoc upon Archie's [Archibald Gordon's] parents? Etc ("*Don't* ever say I told you a word of this." The next day, he told Venetia that "it looks like a clean sweep in Ireland … Dougherty gone, the Aberdeens going (God knows precisely when) and Birrell following – tho' don't say anything about it to him – or to others."

---

201 Ibid. 54.

On the next day, Lady Aberdeen had an interview with Asquith. He had no hesitation in immediately passing on to Venetia the contents of their private conversation, which he described as "one of the most curious & in some ways nerve harrowing interviews." Lady Aberdeen complained that a terrible ruin would be wrought in Ireland if her great work were to be interrupted. Asquith went on:

> "Then she came to the pecuniary aspect of the affair with a most piteous tale and when I pointed out that the Viceroyalty was from its nature a spending and losing concern, … she replied that owing to the War, there would be no Dublin season and so they would be able this next year to make large savings! This roused me I must confess. I said so you want me to continue you in an office, which in the public interest you ought to give up, in order that out of the retrenchments required by a national calamity, you may fill the gaps in your private purse, … She wept copiously poor thing.… in the end I gave them till the beginning of Feb … This is all, I need not say, for your private eye."

In November, this time as a result of a letter he had received from John Redmond, Asquith again sought Venetia's advice about Ireland. Redmond was an MP and leader of the Irish group. He had written to Asquith, "I understand it is seriously contemplated to make a change in the Lord Lieutenancy in Ireland.… I see nothing to be gained from superseding Lord Aberdeen. His removal at the moment would be most unfortunate.… what I would most earnestly urge upon you is that the matter should be at least postponed & and that no announcement should be made at present." This letter, marked "Private", Asquith sent on to Venetia, asking, "What do you say to the enclosed letter from Redmond?" Her views are not known.

However, this was not the end of the Aberdeen saga. On 28 November, Asquith told Venetia, "I had the most extraordinary letter to-day from

Lady Aberdeen. I must show it to you on Monday. It is almost incredible. She wants them to stay on till *April*, & then that he shd. be made an Irish Duke! With a seat perhaps in the Senate of the Home Rule Parliament. They honestly think they are the *homme & femme necessaries,* and that all Ireland (except a few Ulster families) will go into mourning on their departure. I should think there has rarely been a case of such innocent & misguided infatuation."

In January 1915, another domestic political problem needed resolving, namely the appointment of a new chief whip, as Asquith informed Venetia in a series of letters. She was very familiar with the problem, because in June 1914, Lloyd George had raised the issue of the chief whip's position in a private letter to Asquith. Lloyd George suggested that the chief whip's responsibility for dealing with party business in the House of Commons and also with party organisation outside Parliament should be kept separate. Two days later, Asquith felt able to send Venetia this private letter: "I found here the enclosed from LLG[eorge] which, as it is probably the longest letter he has ever written with his own hand, I send you as a curiosity; to be destroyed after you have read it, or if not, to be deposited with other documents in your possession, in some safe & secret receptacle."

In 1915, Montagu favoured the deputy speaker John Whitley for the post of chief whip. Asquith suggested it to Whitley, but he was reluctant to accept, apparently having in mind to be the next speaker. When he and Asquith met, Whitley firmly declined the offer but offered a list of other names. Neil Primrose had been a possible candidate for the India Office in February 1914, but the suggestion that he might become chief whip was vetoed by Venetia. Asquith wrote, "I am glad you told me exactly what you thought about Neil Primrose. I believe – indeed I am sure – you are right." Asquith later told Venetia, "I am sure, with you, that Neil wd. have been a grievous mistake."

Asquith next suggested, faute de mieux, John Gulland for the House and Wedgwood Benn for organisation and the country. He sought Venetia's views. "A daily interview & intimate converse with Gulland has no attraction and I doubt whether I could rely on him.... tell me darling what you think of this." She thought it was uninspiring, as did Lloyd George, but eventually on 21 January Asquith appointed Gulland, though Benn refused.

The question of who should replace Lord Hardinge as viceroy of India was also a subject on which Asquith sought Venetia's views. The matter had been considered in January 1915 because, as Asquith told her, Hardinge had sought an extension of his term of office. The decision was postponed until early summer, and Venetia was told: "All this is very *private*."

The question resurfaced in April, when Asquith told her that Hardinge was to go, whereupon he canvassed a number of possible candidates with her. He ended the letter, "Tell me what your judgement in this is."

A few days later Asquith reported the views of Willingdon (later governor of Madras) on the same subject. "He says Hardinge is too tired & Carmichael too worn out. He thinks Islington wd do alright, probably very well indeed, but suggests Albert Grey – a thoroughly bad choice; a feather-headed loose-tongued gas bag ... although in some ways the best of fellows – is the last kind of head-piece that is wanted in India. Don't you agree?"

Venetia's views are not recorded, but in April 1916, following Hardinge's resignation, Lord Chelmsford became the viceroy.

When the Marquess of Londonderry died on 8 February 1915, Asquith canvassed Venetia's view as to who should succeed him as knight of the garter. On another occasion, he sent her a list of members of his Cabinet, with his own assessment of their abilities, telling her, "This is most secret ... *tell me what you think*. Most darling of darlings..." In the months before the war in 1914, Asquith had also sought Venetia's advice about the political problems of Ireland. The Conservatives, with Carson and Bonar Law at their head, were determined to preserve Ulster as a Protestant province, while Redmond, leader of the Irish group, was firmly opposed. The risk of civil war was very great. The question of whether the army would be used to coerce the opponents of the home rule bill was a matter of controversy. Seely, the war minister, gave the generals, who were Conservative sympathisers, a categorical undertaking in writing, to avoid the risk of a mutiny, that they would not be so used. This was without Asquith's approval, and he publicly repudiated the document. Asquith then decided to take over the War Office himself.

On 30 March, before it was officially announced, he told Venetia of the decision and of Churchill's reaction. "I started the idea of the two offices (ie War Office & Prime Minister) and at once, I need not tell you that Winston's eyes blazed and his polysyllables rolled and his gestures were those of a man possessed."

Maps of the Ulster were exchanged in order to try to agree which areas should be excluded from any agreement. On 11 June, Asquith sent Venetia a copy of one of the maps. "Here is the map which will interest you, and I have written in the percentage of the Protestants and Roman Catholics in each of the counties. I have not yet got an answer to *our* letter [to Carson]."

He followed this up on 14 June. "I had another letter from C[arson] this morning enclosing the long promised map, which is a rather unwieldy affair to look at & hold; I haven't had time yet to examine the details. Did you ever look at yours?"

On 23 June he told Venetia, "I never talked to you yesterday (nor you to me) on political things. I wanted to show you a letter of the Speaker's to whom I have suggested an attempt to bring C[arson] & R[Edmond] into the same room.... I am beginning to form ideas ... nebulous but growing crystalised ... about the future which I must share with you. Talking with no one else, does me so much good."

He went on to seek her approval about who should be members of the committee for antiquarian research, suggesting the names of Lords Bryce and Sheffield. "Don't you think that is a good choice?"

The Ulster problem, however, still continued. "I will tell you", wrote Asquith on 30 June, "of the queer things that are going on in Ulster etc. I wonder if you have thought out any of the problems we discussed on Saturday? I wonder if you also want to talk to me as much as I want to talk to you?"

When the war broke out in August 1914, what had been the confiding of comparatively unimportant private information to Venetia for her approval and agreement, although strictly confidential, was now replaced by a constant succession of the most secret intelligence reports about the conduct of the war. This was done not only in their voluminous correspondence, but often – because of the acute sensitivity of the information – orally. In December 1914, he wrote "I have been looking through Foreign Office telegrams to see if there is anything of interest to tell you. But I can find nothing worth repeating to tell you …"

Asquith still made occasional references to confidential domestic affairs. In March 1915, he was telling Venetia that "here at home all sorts of things are going on and it is quite on the cards (this is *most secret*) that I may create a new office for Ll.George ("Director of War Contracts" or something of the kind) & relieve him of some of his present duties. I shalln't do anything without consulting you, wh. makes it all the more important that we shd. spend tomorrow aft. together. Darling, I have at least a million more things to say…. and (since I mustn't use a messenger) I must send this at once that it may get to you thro. the post by supper time."

But the military secrets were of a different order, and by sharing them with Venetia, Asquith showed himself to be totally irresponsible and lacking in judgement. Only the nature of their relationship is capable of providing any sort of excuse. In August 1914, Venetia was told that French was leaving for Boulogne in a destroyer ("this is *secret*"), that thereafter he was going via Paris to Amiens. He had then set up his headquarters at Le Cateau. An expeditionary force of four divisions was to be sent, of which three divisions had arrived in France and the rest were to follow. Four days after the war started, Asquith told Venetia, "I have had Kitchener & read his instructions to Sir John French as Commander of the Expeditionary force – I have told him to send me a full statement of the composition of the force-regiments & this I will show to you or send to you." He did not mark it secret.

Later in the month, he revealed that the Fifth Division was being sent off to the front, and that this would practically denude Ireland of regulars. When Kitchener wrote to Asquith that the Fourth Division was now crossing to France and that he would talk about the Sixth Division going, his letter was forwarded to Venetia.

Two days later, Kitchener sent Asquith a telegram from French with dire news about the fall of Namur and his decision to retreat. This telegram was forwarded to Venetia accompanied by Asquith's observations. "It is a bad check, to say the least. French has since telegraphed that he wants reinforcements to the extent of 10 per cent – which implies fairly heavy casualties.…" His letter continued, "I wish we had something like a code that we cd. use by the telegraph. This morning, for instance, I longed to let you know before anyone else, what had happened and what was happening."

In August 1914, the result of the German offensive along with feebleness of some of the French Army and its inadequate plan of campaign tactics meant that the British Army was in constant retreat in order to cover its flanks, left unprotected by the withdrawal of its French allies. The new line of the whole Allied army was now to be from Amiens to Rheims. Asquith wasted no time in divulging this highly sensitive information to Venetia, with the admonition "this is *quite secret*".

On 31 August, Asquith wrote: "We had bad news this morning from French. Joffre was in favour of a further retirement of the French armies and wished French to remain practically where he is. French took umbrage at this, and proposes himself, to retire behind the Seine, basing himself on La Rochelle. We all think this quite wrong (all this is *most secret*) …"

The consequence of the retreat was fully spelt out by Asquith. "I am certain it will be found that French has greatly underestimated his total losses which are much more likely to work out at 10,000 than 5,000. In fact if it were otherwise, it is impossible to account for his telegrams in which (*secret*) he speaks of his force shattered & quite unable to take a place, for the time being, in the forefront."

Asquith continued to share with Venetia the movements of the BEF in France. In September, the Allied armies were strongly entrenched on the Aisne, "but Joffre (this too is secret) appears to be contemplating an extended out flanking movement West of *Noyon*."

The number of casualties suffered by the BEF and its state of morale were a constant subject of communications between Asquith and Venetia. In October, the Seventh Division had lost at least 4,000 out of about 12,000 men and 200 officers. The explanation, as Asquith subsequently wrote, "… (what follows is *very private*) was, according to Freddy Guest (who was on a secret mission from French,) that the army was now so reduced by losses that a Corps now numbers little more than a division. The 7th Division, (which was our best), seems to have been badly led by Rawlinson, and Capper, the infantry commander, is said to spend much of his time in a bomb proof hut. (This is all *for you alone*.)"

On 5 October, he told Venetia, "I found when I arrived here this morning the enclosed telegram from Winston who, as you will see, proposes to resign his office to take the command in the field of this great military force! (The army and the marines in Belgium) … I send you the original which I know you won't show to anybody, to add to your collection of *memoires pour server*, with K[itchener]'s marginal annotation."

The idea of Churchill leading the marines in Belgium was treated with some amusement by Asquith, and their intervention in Belgium was only just short of a disaster. The *Times* reported on 14 October that the Belgian government had abandoned Ostend and left for Le Havre, and that the Germans had now occupied Ghent, and Lille.[202]

Asquith continued to tell Venetia the most secret information about troop movements. In January 1915, he wrote: "*Next* (this also *very secret*) an agreement has been come to between Joffre & French for such a rearrangement of troops as will give us the whole of the extreme left flank, and put us in direct touch – without any intervening French – with the Belgians & the sea. This ought to be completed by the first or second week in March." Sometimes he would inform her of the casualties suffered by the BEF. In February, he told her that "they were 10,400 and that Kitchener had reported that in last ten *days* Sir J. French's force had lost one hundred officers and about 2,600 men"

---

202 *Times*, 14 October 1914, 8.

Naval secrets were not immune from disclosure. On 6 August 1914, Asquith revealed to Venetia: "The latest authentic news is that the cruiser *Amphion* which did so well yesterday, has been blown up by mines to-day, and no one saved." Three days later, Venetia was told of the near torpedoing of one of the Navy's best and biggest battleships – the *Monarch* – while at Scapa Flow. This information she was told: "you must not breathe to any one". In September, two cruisers, the *Cressey* and the *Hogue,* went to the assistance of another cruiser, the *Aboukir,* which had been torpedoed in the North Sea, and were themselves torpedoed with considerable loss of life. Asquith wasted no time in reporting this loss to Venetia, adding "the Navy is not doing very well just now: there are nearly ½ a dozen German cruisers – which are at large on the high seas & in all parts of the world, are sinking or capturing British merchantmen. Things came almost to a climax at the Cabinet today, when we learnt that the New Zealanders absolutely decline to despatch their expeditionary force … unless we can provide them with a sufficiently powerful escort to convey them in safety from Wellington to Adelaide."

In October 1914, the admiralty had succeeded in sending three submarines all the way into the Baltic "to deal havoc among the German warships there". This information, as Asquith told Venetia, "is very secret". This was not the only plan to attack the Germans in their homeland. On 24 October, Asquith wrote:

> "(Most secret) … the plan I have long been urging is about to come off. That is to say that to-day, a certain number of old & specially prepared ships go to within about 30 miles of Heligoland, protected by destroyers & cruisers. From there, as from a springboard, a detachment of sea planes, will fly straight for Cuxhaven, spy out all the German preparations there & in the Kiel Canal; make havoc, if they can, of the Zeppelins & their sheds; & return (if they can) to their ships…. this is far the most romantic & adventurous side of modern war. *Nobody* knows of this – except W[inston] and myself."

It was only a few days later that Asquith reported another naval disaster, the mining of the super dreadnought *Audacious* off the coast of Northern Ireland. To begin with, Asquith only hinted at what had happened. "Winston came here before lunch in a rather sombre mood. Strictly between you & me, he has suffered a dreadful calamity on the sea which I *dare* not describe, lest by chance my letter should go wrong; it is known only to him & me and for a long time will, & must be kept secret."

His resolve to keep the matter a secret, known only to himself and Winston, did not last long because on the very next day he was able to tell Venetia:

> "The disaster of wh. I wrote in veiled language yesterday, was the sinking of the *Audacious* ... one of the best and newest of the super dreadnoughts ... it is far the worst calamity the Navy has so far suffered ... after a rather heated discussion in the Cabinet this morning, we resolved *not* to make public this loss at the moment.... Of course you will say nothing about the *Audacious,* till it is public property."

Asquith had already told Venetia about the conflicting views as to the best approach to ending the stalemate in France and that it had been decided that an "Eastern" solution should be adopted. But, while she knew of the general strategy, she was unaware of the tactical details until in February 1915 he revealed that "the whole situation in the Near East may be transformed if the bombardment of the Dardanelles by our ships next week (*Secret*) goes well. It is a great experiment." He continued, "the only exciting thing in prospect (after seeing you on Friday) is what will happen in the Dardanelles next week. This, as I said, is supposed to be a secret, and indeed I believe it isn't known to some members of the Cabinet ... it is full of uncertainties ... naturally I shall tell you *everything*....This is all for *yourself alone.*"

A day or two later, he informed her, "A secret telegram came this morning which has only been seen by Winston, Grey, K[itchener] & me." This was all about Gallipoli, and Venetia was kept fully in the picture as to what had happened and what was going to happen. This he described as "a well kept secret" but added "I always want you to know everything".

In March, he told her of a secret telegram which announced that the Greeks were going to send three divisions of troops to Gallipoli and added, "It is really *far* the most interesting moment up to now in the War, & I long to talk it all over with you, my dearest and wisest."

The situation in the Dardanelles had begun to take a turn for the worse, as Venetia was informed shortly before midnight on 24 March. And in April, when the Dardanelles operation continued to prove abortive, Asquith sought Venetia's view about the best way forward.

Attempts to persuade neutral countries to join the Allied side were a constant subject of discussion at the Cabinet, as Asquith reported to Venetia. "Meanwhile (but this is secret) the Portuguese offer to supply a large number of *mitrailleuses* & about 10,000 horses & 3 or 4000 troops. This will make them belligerents on our side." Turkey had entered the war on the German side in November 1914, but it was hoped that other Balkan countries would join the Allies. In November 1914, Asquith revealed that "desperate measures are being made to find some territorial formula which will bring Bulgaria & Romania into the fighting line alongside of Serbia & Greece. It is no easy job."

As the War continued through the spring of 1915, there was no letting up of the secrets which Asquith revealed about the neutrals. In March he had told her:

> "in regard to things abroad there have emerged two most infernal problems.... what I tell you about them is *most secret*. The first is that there are significant indications that before very long Italy may come in on the side of the allies.... the other question, (and this is, if possible, *more secret*) is the future of Constantinople & the Straits. It has become quite clear that Russia plans to incorporate them in her own Empire ... I really don't know how it

will be viewed in France or this country; it is of course a complete reversal of our old traditional policy.... Think over these things & let me have your thoughts."

The question of inducing the neutrals to join the Allied side continued to occupy the government. On 27 March 1915, Asquith wrote: "If in addition we cd rope in both Italy & Bulgaria (Austria being now almost *in extremis*) we ought to be within sight of the end of the war. This, I am afraid, is the only *mundane* thing I have to contribute ... and you told me yesterday that you liked that & the *other* to be mixed like a salad."

The fact that Asquith confided the most secret information both before and during the war to Venetia – then simply a young civilian, politically somewhat unsophisticated, and lacking any military experience or expertise – and that he further sought out and relied on her advice suggests a deeply intimate relationship between them.

CHAPTER NINE

The Conspiracy of Silence

"the dog which didn't bark"

Autobiographies and biographies by relatives of the subject are not expected to paint a picture of "warts and all", but if, as in the case of Asquith, they are intended to be a serious record of an illustrious life, it is, to say the least, very surprising that Venetia's name has been simply airbrushed out of the family history. No great significance, perhaps, is to be drawn from the absence of her letters to him which no longer exist. It is not clear how they came to be missing. But the family have written a good deal about Asquith, as he himself has done, and they have published well over a dozen diaries and memoirs of the time. With them it is possible, without the letters, for the reader to form an educated assessment of his career and character. While others, such as Jenkins, Clifford, and Koss, have written distinguished biographies, probably the most authoritative biography is that written jointly by J.A. Spender and Asquith's son Cyril, his youngest by his first wife, who later became a law lord. His book is called *Life of Lord Oxford and Asquith*.

It was published in two volumes in 1932 and runs, in all, to some 750 pages. It is *the* authorised biography. At the time they wrote their book, Asquith had been dead for some four years, but Margot was still alive, as were Violet and Cyril's two other brothers. And so was Venetia, her sister Sylvia Henley, and a large number of colleagues who had known Asquith politically. Many friends were also still alive who had known them both socially. The biography *Life of Lord Oxford and Asquith* is widely cast. But the reader who looks to the book for any mention of Asquith's friendship with Venetia will be sadly disappointed.

In all the pages of this definitive biography, there are only two brief references to the very existence of Venetia. The first, in volume one, reads: "He discovered a need for some receptive and sympathetic female intelligence outside the circle of his family, to which he could communicate, as a matter of routine, the spontaneous outflow of thought or humour, of fancy or emotion. A whole succession of women friends responded to this need – Venetia Stanley and latterly Mrs Harrisson may be cited as examples."[203] The second reference is in volume two, where the authors describe a visit by Asquith to stay with the Sheffields at Penrhos, near Holyhead (one of Sheffield's country houses), in 1914. "His [Asquith's] wife remained in London but he wrote to her every day and his letters speak of picnics on the sea shore with the Snowden range in full view, of cheerful small talk with friends and fellow guests, of daily golf." The book continues, "On 29 May, he wrote to Margot. 'I went to the links at Holyhead yesterday which are very interesting, and played one ball, the local professional and Venetia (the Hon Venetia Stanley) playing the other....'"[204] Why he felt it necessary to explain to his wife who Venetia was, remains something of a mystery. Asquith himself was no more forthcoming. In April 1915, he had sent Venctia what he described as a "chapter of autobiography":

> "I knew what an angel of comfort and help she had shown herself to Violet. In the second general election of that year (Nov and Dec 1910) she and Violet and I had great "fun" travelling about together to meetings, the occasion I best remember being our visit to Bluey's [Harold Baker, MP] constituency of Accrington, and our evening afterwards in the grim and frostbitten

---

203 Spender, i. 217.

204 Spender, ii. 50.

atmosphere of Shuttleworth and Gawsthorpe. So things went on with long intervals of absence and separation; but always when we came together again, we resumed without effort, as though it had never been broken off, the delightful attitude of true companionship. The only new things I noticed in particular were her interest and knowledge of poetry, and her really remarkable memory not only for words but for things and places.

The first stage of our intimacy (in which there was not a touch of romance and hardly of sentiment) came to its climax when I went to Sicily with Montagu as a companion, I think at the end of 1911 or beginning of 1912. Violet and Venetia joined us there, and we had together one of the most interesting and delightful fortnights in all our lives. It was when we got back to England and I was spending most of my Sundays in the late winter and early spring at a house lent to me on the outskirts of the New Forest (I remember it was on the eve of the Coal Strike which gave me one of the most trying experiences – up to then – of my public life) that she came down with us for the usual "weekend."

I was sitting with her in the dining room on Sunday morning – the others being out in the garden or walking – and we were talking and laughing just on our old accustomed terms. Suddenly, in a single instant, without premonition on my part or any challenge on hers, the scales dropped from my eyes, the familiar features & smile & gestures & words assumed an absolutely new perspective; what had been completely hidden from me in a flash half-revealed, and I dimly felt, hardly knowing, not at all understanding it, that I had come to a turning point in my life."

Not a single word of this rather touching account of the beginning of their friendship is to be found in any of Asquith's or his family's memoirs.

Asquith wrote a number of autobiographies or memoirs. There are two volumes of *Memories and Reflections*. They were published in September 1928. Together they run to some 450 pages. There is no reference to Venetia in either volume.[205] In 1926 he had published two volumes of *Fifty Years of Parliament*. They run, in all, to some 520 pages. No mention of Venetia appears.[206] *Letters from Lord Oxford to a Friend* start in June 1915. They were published in two volumes in 1933 and 1934. Although they were, in fact, addressed to Hilda Harrisson, her name does not appear in the book. The editor, Desmond MacCarthy, wrote in the introduction, "Like all men of strongly masculine temperament, women were important in his [Asquith's] life … the lady of the letters stood apart from the main current of his life. In herself, and also in this respect, she [i.e. Hilda] was evidently the intimate woman-friend he needed."[207]

Asquith fully described his relationship with Hilda. "In June 1915, I formed a new friendship to which I have since been greatly indebted – my acquaintance with her ripened after the death of her husband (he was killed in 1917) when in the course of 1918–1919 … we became regular and intimate correspondents."[208]

The correspondence continued until 1927. Over a period of some twelve years, it amounted on average to little more than once a month, and the contrast between his letters to her and his letters to Venetia could not be more marked. Totally absent in the letters to Hilda is any hint of the passionate or amorous expressions which are the hallmark

---

205 *Memories.*

206 Earl of Oxford and Asquith, *Fifty Years of Parliament* (London: Cassell and Company Ltd., London, 1926).

207 H.H.A. *Letters from Lord Oxford to a Friend.* i. xi.

208 *Memories*, ii. 156.

of his correspondence with Venetia. The fact that Asquith was happy for Hilda's name to appear in his memoirs, while Venetia's very existence is wholly ignored, speaks volumes about the relationship between him and Venetia.

Margot was no more forthcoming, although she was later to claim that she was well aware of Asquith's attachment to Venetia. She wrote to Montagu in April 1915: "Our relationship [Asquith with Margot] is absolutely unique. Every night, however late, I go and sit on his knee in my nightgown and we tell each other everything … he shows me *all* his letters and all Venetia's and tells me every secret, things he tells no one in the world." It is self-evident from the letters themselves that she was deluding herself. Asquith wrote many of his letters not only at different times but also from all sorts of different places, to which Margot had no access. He wrote on trains, in the House of Commons, at Cabinet meetings, and at War Council meetings, sometimes very late at night, or when he was staying away, alone. He frequently gave Venetia the most secret information which, as he told her, he had not shared with others. Clearly Margot was aware that Asquith was writing to Venetia, but equally clearly, she simply had no idea of the frequency of the correspondence, nor of the passionate nature of the letters, nor of the confidential information which they contained. In 1907, she had famously described Venetia as being enrolled into his "little harem", but it is straining credulity to believe that he conducted his lengthy affair with Venetia with the full knowledge or approval of Margot.

A similar view was expressed by Emma Tennant, who was a relative of Margot's:

> "The trouble is he [Asquith] no longer confides anything in his wife. Venetia who has tucked a letter into her dress before giving that unpleasant smile and vanishing … she is the recipient of the most weighty of the Prime Minister's confidences. He writes to her three times a day, from the House of Commons; from weekends at "The Wharf"; from his bedroom

> whence he has long been banished by Margot ... He sends her everything – military secrets, declarations of an undying love, childish games and puzzles – to this clever, ungainly girl. Margot may not be capable of guessing the extent of her husband's correspondence with Miss Stanley ..."[209]

Margot made every effort to restrict knowledge of his affair with Venetia "to the smallest possible circle and to put the best construction on it". She sent a memorandum to Spender when he was writing his biography of Asquith in 1932, minimising the relationship between Asquith and Venetia and playing up the friendship which he had with Hilda. His letters to Hilda had recently been published. Spender did not, in fact, use the memorandum or refer to the three women, but Margot's memorandum shows how keen she was to play down the Asquith-Venetia relationship, even some twenty years after it started.[210] In her two autobiographies of over six hundred pages, there is no mention of Venetia, nor is there in *More Memories*, published in 1933.

Elsewhere Margot does mention Venetia, but in these terms:

> "It was not until fifteen years after our marriage that he formed the two friendships with women that gave him the most pleasure in life. The first was Venetia Stanley – his daughter Violet's greatest friend – who before her marriage spent most of her holidays with us in Scotland and elsewhere. Her parents, Lord and Lady Sheffield, were intimate friends of ours, and when I was ill the Asquith children had long visits to the Sheffield family at Penrhos. I suffered so much from my confinements that I seldom accompanied them but both Venetia and her sister Sylvia became friends of mine and it was only years later that my husband developed a deep affection

---

209 Emma Tennant, *Strangers* (London: Vintage, 1999), 24–25.
210 Bennett. *252.*

for Venetia. Her cleverness, enterprise and good humour, as well as her talent for writing letters and genuine affection attracted him. But when she married our secretary Edwin Montagu who joined Mr Lloyd George when we left Downing Street, she moved in a different circle and we saw little of her."[211]

Of Hilda, Margot wrote:

"His other woman friend, whom he saw and whom he corresponded with till the end of his life, was Hilda Harrisson. She lived near my sister … so we had every opportunity of meeting her. Mrs Harrisson's husband was killed in the war and she was left with two small children and little money.… My husband appreciated her devotion, and, her companionship was a refreshing rest from the turmoil of Downing Street. Her equability of temper, Liberalism, and sincerity endeared her to both of us. They played bridge, and golf and chess together at a time when political events made us unhappy. I was only too glad to see the pleasure he took in her letters and companionship. H.H always told me when she intended to go for motor drives or meet him in London and never at any time concealed her devotion to him.… After the confidence he had shown in me in our early married life, I felt it would have been a lack of generosity to have withheld mine when in his later years he developed a lasting affection for Hilda Harrisson."[212]

---

211 Margot Asquith, *Off The Record* (London: Frederick Muller Ltd., 1943), 121.

212 *Margot*, 254-255.

Nor were Margot's memoirs any more informative. Cynthia, too, "violently inked over all references [to Asquith's behaviour] in her diary."[213]

The Asquiths seem to have had a penchant for keeping secret information which they found disagreeable to record. Margot lost three children at birth, one in 1899, one in 1900, and the other in 1906. Not only do they not appear in the family tree in some biographies, which has no particular significance, but the fact appears nowhere in any of the Asquith memoirs or biographies save in Violet's diaries. On 29 December 1906, she wrote to Venetia:

> "Darling Venetia – I loved getting your letter. I know you will realise what we are all going through just now. I was wired for on Monday morning & arrived in an anguish of fear to find M[argot] very ill. The baby was born at 3 that afternoon (Xmas Eve) very tiny and fragile from coming so much too soon but so vital & well-developed that the Drs were very hopeful … it was a boy which I longed for…. We went to bed quite happily … leaving the nurse triumphantly sanguine & it died at 6 the next morning…. Margot never saw it."[214]

It thus appears that the Asquith family have taken a Trappist vow of silence in relation to Venetia and attempted to remove any reference to her from their memoirs. There is perhaps only one conclusion to be drawn.

---

213 Nicola Beauman, *Cynthia Asquith* (Hamish Hamilton, 1987), 195.
214 *Lantern Slides*, 121.

CHAPTER TEN

Opportunities

One of the final strands in the argument is whether there was, in the words of Lord Atkin, "the opportunity for misconduct"? The letters again give a full history and description of their frequent meetings. In December 1908, Asquith had written to Violet, "I am living a most virtuous life (perhaps in the absence of temptation)". He had not yet embarked on his love affair with Venetia. There were, of course, times when Venetia would accompany him to some public occasion, but these fade into insignificance compared with the frequency of their private trysts. That he regarded their meetings as a matter of very great significance is borne out by the constant references to his disappointment when they could not meet.

There was a regular arrangement that they would meet on Fridays when they would often go out in Asquith's car, but visits were not confined to any particular day. A typical description of their meetings can be found in the letters. "I should be deeply depressed about Friday", wrote Asquith on 26 February 1914, "and cursing that infernal soldier with imprecations [history does not relate the circumstances] … were it not that I can look back on our delicious time together yesterday & forward to Saturday and Sunday. All the same, I hate to break the continuity of our Fridays, which have now gone on so long and been so uniformly full of happy hours." "I hope we shall meet at dinner tomorrow night. Can I come Wed before dinner?"[215] "It was delicious

---
215 Ibid. 53.

having you last night though the conditions might have been better." "… solace and joy, as the thought of you and our delicious drive has been all thro' the wet dreary Sunday at the Wharf …" "Short as it was – far too short – I thought we had a delicious time and the drive back today was a thing to remember."

The letters referring to their meetings were as frequent as the rest of their correspondence. It appears from what he wrote that they met privately on well over a hundred occasions. They have a certain air of repetition, but it is impossible not to feel the strength of the emotion which Asquith demonstrated.

Above all, the letters need to be looked at in the context that while these romantic outings were going on, Asquith was in charge of a country, involved in a war to the death.

"Yes, we had a *divine* time all too short, tho' longer than one could have hoped.…" "Yesterday was a particularly dreary day – except for our divine time together for wh I bless you. I shall see you tonight?" "… between 6 & 7 every cloud was lifted (you were never more dear) and later on at the Opera … I felt more than happy. This time at any rate I loved your dress, and even my most critical scrutiny, in other respects, was more than satisfied." "It was heavenly to have a 2 hours respite and real companionship with you today." "I exercised real self denial, darling in regard to your suggestion that I should join you at dinner. I hate even the possibility of gossip about us. It was heavenly to be with you for half an hour. I will come tomorrow at or soon after 5.30." "Wednesday night & yest. afternoon are memories which will never fade."

"I was more touched than I can say by the little piece of white heather and what you wrote about it.… It seems a whole century since our last broken half hour on Thursday, but I shall never forget a week ago tonight." "But unless Fate is very unkind I shall, all the same, hope to come to you, Saturday, and see you – perhaps in your new striped dress, not the 'yellow peril'" "I am still hoping to see you Friday or Saturday.… and I might put myself on for Mells [the Somerset country house of Sir John and Lady Horner] this Sunday. Would you like that? or rather wait for the next? … it is doubtful whether I shall be able to be away for 24 hours …" "And tho' yesterday was rather broken up, Saturday was a golden day & I shall never forget (will you?) the hours we spent together, under the leaden sky & dripping rain, with the glimpses of heather & constant change of pine and oak, and (what was worth more than everything outside) the close real deep understanding & love …"

In September, Asquith wrote, "I motored down alone to Hackwood [in Hampshire, leased in Asquith's name by Curzon] along that road (thro' Egham &c) which you and I know so well, and I thought of those heavenly journies: when shall we have another?"

As the relationship got more intense, so too did the extravagance of the correspondence, which managed to stifle the chilling effect of the war. "Do you remember our sunset on Friday, & Hampton Court in the gloaming, and dimly lighted London …?" A few days earlier, *H.M.S. Pathfinder*, a light cruiser of 2,300 tons, had struck a mine and had sunk with heavy loss of life.[216] In France, there was a series of gigantic battles on the Marne, which the *Times* correspondent described as "a whole campaign as it were, crowded into a single day."[217] But Asquith continued to write, "Can we ever forget those divine hours on Saturday and Sunday? They are part of us both, beyond the reach of chance or change – an ineffaceable memory – the little slope with the long grass, and the dogs in attendance, and the delicious alternations of silence & speech; and later on, the twilight on the wooden bench in the garden, with the moon & the evening star & the Great Bear.… the price of absence & separation is heavy indeed, but not too heavy if (as I firmly believe) there is even more for us in the future than there has been in the past."

While Asquith and Venetia were enjoying this romantic weekend, the war in France and Belgium was not going well, as the *Times* reported on 11 October. Antwerp had fallen to the Germans, who were now

---

216 *Times*, 6 September 1914, 1.

217 Ibid., 14 September 1914, 8.

advancing on Ostend. A British Brigade was cut off in Holland.[218] On 21 October, there was a report of heavy fighting near Ypres with the Germans advancing.[219]

This did not prevent Asquith from spending much of his time with Venetia. He wrote, "It was really a piece of heavenly luck in this ill starred crisis-riddled year to have had 3 whole days with you." "But I loved much more your wish that I was in your little room, and that we could have had another of those heavenly hours wh. are the best things in life." How he had enough free time both to write these romantic letters and also to be able to get away from the centre of government with such regularity, particularly during the war, enjoying "delicious drives" with Venetia, is something of a mystery.

His letters continued in the same vein. "But it would be the height of ingratitude to fortune not to be thankful for the last 48 hours. Our drive on Sat, I am sure we shall both agree was one to be always remembered; even Canterbury Cathedral had its alleviating moments; and the gloaming as we came back from Rye, & still more our delicious hour before dinner, made Sunday a red letter day."

While Asquith and Venetia were driving round Kent, the reports from France were of incessant German attacks. "They [the Germans] have renewed their attacks again and again, undismayed by the heavy losses inflicted upon them. For more than a month past they have been thundering at our lines with shell and shrapnel; they have thrown great masses of infantry upon our trenches."[220]

"I hope you won't exclude Jan 2nd at Walmer [Asquith's weekend retreat] from the sphere of possibility or probability. There is no difficulty about room. And it would be so delicious to spend 48 hours together in new and nice surroundings –" "Looking back, I can hardly remember a day out of 365 when I have not either written to you or seen you, or done both." "But might not *Wed* be possible, if I came not much later than 2 &

---

218 *Times*, 11 October 1914, 1.

219 Ibid., 21 October 1914, 7.

220 *Times*, 16 November 1914, 8.

picked you up & we tried 'fresh woods' in the direction of Epping Forest. I *must* see you at least *twice* in every week: otherwise I shall starve."

He obviously meant it seriously, because four days later he told Venetia that he had postponed his interview with the King until noon in order that "we might have the hour, 10.30 to 11.30 together." On 1 February1915, he suggested "… we will have a good time together tomorrow", which they obviously did, because on 3 February he reminded her, "We had a heavenly hour together yesterday; you were very sweet to me, though once or twice a trifle elusive. But I never loved you more …"

The correspondence was maintained throughout the spring. In March, he wrote "My own most dearly and entirely beloved, I had the most heavenly time with you before dinner (you were never more dear) and it was an unspeakable joy to see you at & after dinner, more beautiful than I have ever seen you …" The drives continued. "Tomorrow – (unless the Heavens fall) I shall come to you in the motor at Mansfield St [the town house of Lord Sheffield] between 5.45 & 6 and we will have one of our divine drives … and we will make plans for the following days." "The next day he wrote, "We had a heavenly drive this afternoon … hadn't we? You were divine as you always are …" He summed up the pleasure of their drives together when he wrote, "I will undertake to say, that in the hundred or more of our drives, there has been a greater interchange of 'Fun' in the best and widest sense, than has ever happened, in our time, or perhaps my time, between any man and any woman."

CHAPTER ELEVEN

The Verdict

It is clear that the evidence of the witnesses is somewhat contradictory. Diana's views are a good example. From such testimony alone, it is not possible to form a firm conclusion about the relationship. But when taking into account the other factors, namely the passion of the correspondence, the myriad confidences expressed therein, the reliance on Venetia for advice (just like a married couple), the frequency of their meetings, the descriptions of them, the subsequent adultery of Venetia with a number of lovers, and the remarkable silence of the Asquith memoirs, the picture becomes tolerably clear.

One more piece of evidence completes that picture. Asquith had had five children by Helen and five by Margot, three of whom died at childbirth. For Margot, pregnancy was a nightmare. Her sister Laura had died giving birth to a son, and Margot was haunted by the prospect of another pregnancy for herself.

After her marriage to Asquith in May 1894, children followed in quick succession. Her first child was a daughter, born in May 1895. She died after a few hours. The effect on Margot was to leave her shattered. Postnatal depression set in, and sleeplessness became part of her life. In February 1897, Margot gave birth to a healthy child, Elizabeth. The arrival of the child not only improved Margot's health, but increased her happiness.

In early 1900, Margot lost a second baby and was again very ill. She had difficulty in eating and suffered from faintness and depression. In

November 1902, she gave birth prematurely to a son, Anthony, who survived. Yet again, in December 1906, when Margot was 40, she gave birth to a son who died within a few hours, graphically described by Violet.[221] Postnatal depression, for which there was no alleviation but time, brought on the insomnia she was so afraid of. Once again she entered the long, dark, and lonely tunnel in which fear, pain, and despair were her only companions. She had operations for a number of ailments and continued to suffer from depression, nausea, and stomach pains.

As a result, in 1907 the doctors decided that they must take a firm line: "There must be no more children – not the slightest risk must be taken."[222] While the decision no doubt had its effect on Margot, for Asquith himself it was to lead to serious consequences. Here was a man aged 55, who had already conceived ten children. He was in the prime of life, vigorous, virile and (as his contemporaries vouchsafed) attractive to and attracted by young women, but who was now to be banished from the marriage bed and confined to sleeping apart from his wife in a separate bedroom. Why, then, should it occasion even the slightest surprise if within a few years he should seek solace from a young, attractive woman like Venetia, who was not only half Margot's age, but subsequently to be the mistress of others, in order to escape from his celibate life?

This surely is the final piece in the puzzle. A distinguished judge once said, "Circumstantial evidence is very often the best. It is evidence of surrounding circumstances, which by undesigned co-incidence, is capable of proving a proposition with the accuracy of mathematics."[223]

Therefore, from the evidence – both individually and cumulatively – one is driven to the inexorable conclusion that the relationship between Asquith and Venetia was indeed sexual. No judge or jury looking at *all* the evidence could reasonably reach any other verdict.

---

221 *Lantern Slides*, 121.

222 Bennett, 174.

223 Lord Chief Justice Hewart, *Taylor v R, 21 Criminal Appeal Reports*, paragraph 20 at 21.